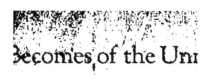

Becomes of the Un

C000127079

BY

ALBERTA S. B. GUIBORD, M. D.
Psychiatrist Church Home Society
Assistant Physician Boston State Hospital

AND

IDA R. PARKER
Associate Director Research Bureau on
Social Case Work

RESEARCH BUREAU ON SOCIAL CASE WORK
400 BOYLSTON STREET, BOSTON
1922

CONTENTS

SECTION 2

III

WHAT BECOMES OF THE UNMARRIED MOTHER?

INTRODUCTION

Motherhood without marriage is such a frank departure from the social code of civilized peoples, it is so inevitably linked up with the idea of disgrace we cannot wonder that the most compelling consideration of the girl who finds herself in this experience is to keep it a secret. Naturally the girl's family when cognizant of the fact has the same compulsion to conceal it. The social worker or other person who seeks to help the girl through the trying time of confinement and subsequent return to community life is virtually bound, in the interests of her charge, to abet the policy of secrecy.

As a result of this single incentive to hide the experience from the world and to foster the pretense that nothing has happened, the unmarried mother as such soon loses her identity even to those who have known her most intimately during her period of storm and stress. Except for an occasional case known here and there to some individual, we have little dependable information as to what eventually becomes of girls who have borne a child without sanction of law or church and without even a sign of recognition from the partner who had an equal share in bringing them into this difficult situation.

We can of course readily call to mind from the books of our earlier and more recent reading the stories of the after-lives of unmarried mothers. But these accounts have been deliberately worked up for artistic or emotional effect on the reader. Whether they represent the facts of real life we do not know, because we have no fund of information with which to compare them. Do girls react to this experience by desperate recourse to infanticide as Hettie Sorrell in *Adam Bede*, by suicide as Effie Bright in *If Winter Comes*, by stoical withdrawal from the world as Hester Prynne in *The Scarlet Letter*, by the comparatively easy shifting of the burden to someone else as Noel Pierson in *Saint's Progress*, or do they react in some entirely different way?

The agencies and institutions who have dealt with unmarried mothers for years have as yet little collective information to offer on this subject. Their pressing obligation to care for a constantly incoming stream of current cases leaves them little opportunity to follow up the cases that have passed out of active care. There is naturally little incentive for a girl to seek on her own initiative to continue a relationship which, however acceptable it may have been at the time of her extreme need, is a constant reminder of an experience which she wishes to forget herself and to have others forget. Friendly relations between individual workers and particular girls are of course in many instances maintained for a long time. Often this friendly relationship is the strongest influence in the social readjustment of the girl. The point we wish to make is that there has not been any such conscientious and scientific attempt to discover the outcome or the effects of motherhood without marriage as there has been to discover its causation.

Yet for purely practical and immediate purposes it would seem important to know how the unmarried mother turns out. Today, social agencies spend largely of time, money, and effort in caring for these girls. Unquestionably they aim to do the very best for each and to place her in the way of "making good." Is it not then important to inquire whether or not she does "make good"—whether the plan made for her has been as wise and effective as possible, or whether by checking up the outcome with the original plan it might not be possible to see ways of improving the treatment so as to secure a greater degree of success in handling later cases? This much, it would seem, every agency or institution ought to require itself to do, not only to give it a scientific pride in its work but also to justify its claim on the public for support.

But there is a deeper reason for seeking to find out what becomes of the unmarried mother; namely, for the bearing the information might have on the broad social question of unmarried motherhood and illegitimacy. Whether motherhood without marriage tends to have ultimately a constructive, a destructive, or no apparent effect on the after-life of the girl, ought to have some weight in the appraisement of its social significance and

6

hence some weight in the determination of the public attitude and the public policy regarding it. The public attitude today is universally condemnatory. It is, to be sure, not a deliberately reasoned condemnation, but a predetermined mental set. Without looking at the evidence in the case it automatically stamps the unmarried mother an "unworthy character." This mechanical condemnation imposes a substantial handicap on both the mother and the child in many ways, but chiefly in that it operates to keep them both, more particularly the child, out of the more favorable conditions of living.

With the question of the illegitimate child as such this paper has no special concern. It will be touched only in so far as the history of the child is bound up with the subsequent history of the mother. The subject has been dealt with by others, notably in the thoroughgoing study made by the United States Children's Bureau, 1921, *Illegitimacy As a Child Welfare Problem.* This study shows beyond shadow of doubt that the illegitimate child has not an equal chance physically, morally, or mentally with the legitimate child to grow into normal adulthood. Unquestionably the handicap which the illegitimate child carries arises out of more than one source, but one of the most apparent is the condemnatory attitude which society holds toward the unmarried mother because it conduces to concealment and repudiation. In all probability the child's handicap will not be lifted until the public attitude towards the mother is changed. That the public attitude should be changed we do not assert. We do not know whether it should or not; but whatever the public attitude, it ought to be based on the evidence existing today rather than on prejudice inherited from past ages.

The first step toward arriving at a reasoned attitude is, self-evidently, to examine all the factors involved: to find out first who the unmarried mothers are and then how they react to the experience—how they turn out in view of it. To find out who they are is comparatively easy because of the physiological crisis which brings them all to a state of helplessness and the statutory requirement which lists them all in the public records.[1] A good

[1] Violation of this statute is common as shown in the study of the United States Children's Bureau already cited.

deal of data on this subject already is at hand. In Kammerer's book, *The Unmarried Mother,* the personal histories of 500 cases are reported in considerable detail. In the Children's Bureau study the personal histories of nearly one thousand cases were reviewed and the findings tabulated. The following is quoted from the chapter on *Conclusions,* p. 71, of this publication:

"* * * a large number of cases (unmarried mothers) come from homes in which there is poverty, dependency, alcoholism, immorality, absence of parental supervision or even in some instances encouragement of misconduct. In other cases she had no home * * * *. Significant also are lack of moral training, ignorance of the dangers involved in disregard of the safeguards that have been built up through social conventions, and too great suggestibility or other weakness of character. One of the generally recognized factors in delinquency of this kind is mental subnormality which results in lack of judgment and self control." Obviously this is not the whole story in view of the fact that there are some unmarried mothers in whom none of the enumerated factors operate and conversely not all girls in whom they do operate become unmarried mothers. Nevertheless, it is safe to say, that all who are well acquainted with the subject agree in the main with the conclusion quoted as to who the girls are that carry through to this completed phase of sex delinquency: not clear visioned, strong-willed transgressors who deliberately elect the experience for themselves, but girls who, for one reason or another, lack the wisdom, the foresight, and the self-directing power to keep themselves out of it; or, possibly in some cases, girls whose moral or religious scruples forbid them to interfere with a generative process.

To find out how the unmarried mother turns out is, for the reason already pointed out, a more difficult task. It can readily be seen that for such an inquiry to have scientific value it should embrace a large number of cases; cover a long period of time, enough at least for the experience to have exerted its maximum effect; and most of all, it should take into account only those cases who have been previously studied and about whom the facts are known and recorded in respect to personal history, family history, and physical and mental make-up. Without such initial

8

data as a basis for comparison it would be very difficult to say whether a girl appeared to be better, worse, or unchanged after the experience. Bearing all this in mind, the writers venture to offer a follow-up study, not because it fulfils all the requirements enumerated, but in the hope that even a small study such as this may show something of value and pave the way to more extensive study by others.

This study deals with 82 unmarried mothers whose babies were born during the period between November, 1914 and July, 1918. The mothers were distributed at this time variously under the care of two private maternity homes, four private social agencies, and one private obstetrical hospital. They find place in this study because they were all brought to one of the writers for mental examination.

The study divides naturally into two parts: (I) The INITIAL OR INTRODUCTORY STUDY made by Dr. Guibord from data obtained at the time of the mental examination directly from the girls themselves and from the records of the agencies and (II) the FOLLOW-UP STUDY of the cases introduced in part I made by Miss Parker in 1921-22. It includes an analysis of the methods of the social management or treatment of the mothers and the data obtained from the follow-up investigation five years, approximately, after the birth of the respective children. Each part is essentially an individual writing, therefore opinions expressed in one part do not necessarily bind the writer of the other part. A summary and tables at the end aim to show, (a) the present social satus of the subjects as compared with the social status at the time of the pregnancy with which this paper is concerned, that is to say, whether as judged by social criteria they are better, worse, or the same; and (b) the apparent result to the community, that is to say, whether by the occurrence of these illegitimate pregnancies the community has been injured or not appreciably affected.

This study fails to fulfil the requirements of scientific value enumerated above in the following particulars: (1) It does not embrace a large number of cases; furthermore, the group is in all probability, not a representative one for, as explained later, the girls in this study were for the most part special problem

9

cases. (2) It does not cover a long period of time, five years being the maximum interval. Yet this fact undoubtedly has afforded the advantage of locating a larger number of individuals than would have been located had the follow-up investigation been longer deferred. Even at the end of this comparatively short period it has been difficult to get at the information; in eight cases it has been impossible. (3) It is not as complete in all particulars of the initial history as it should be, more especially in the items of family history and physical examination. The reason for this will presently appear.

I. THE INITIAL STUDY

The initial study aims to supply a general size-up or picture of the group. It does not purport to be an intensive study of the unmarried mother or of the etiology of motherhood without marriage. These subjects have received scientific attention notably in the study of Kammerer and that of the Children's Bureau. It aims merely to provide the necessary background for the follow-up presentation. It will therefore touch in as brief and condensed a manner as feasible only certain features which seem to have direct bearing on the subsequent reactions, namely: (A) the mental examination, (B) some items of the personal history, (C) the physical examination, (D) the family history. Summaries or tables, with comment or without, will be utilized as seems most conducive to clearness.

A. MENTAL EXAMINATION.

This is made the most conspicuous topic of the initial study because of its relation to behavior, because in this particular our records are most nearly complete, and because mental diagnosis, particularly in its psychometric aspect, seems to provide the nearest approach to a common standard for estimating the subsequent career of the subjects.

The mental examination was sought by a social worker of the agency that had the girl in care as an aid to a better understanding of the girl in the hope of making a satisfactory program for her future. With one or two exceptions the examination was sought because the girl in question was a particular problem in respect to some difficulty of adaptation at the moment, some strikingly atypical personal characteristic, or some unusual feature in her past history. It will therefore be seen, as has been already pointed out, that this is a group of special cases.

The examination was made for the most part at the maternity home or the hospital in which the girls were awaiting confinement or soon after it had occurred. A few were examined at the psychiatrist's office, a few at a certain out-patient clinic. Examination at this out-patient clinic was very soon discon-

11

tinued because the delay and publicity necessarily entailed were found to be mentally upsetting to the subjects. With the exception of one girl who refused test and one who was incapable because of emotional disturbance, the cooperation in the mental examination was cordial.

The mental examination consisted first, of determination of the intelligence grade by the Stanford Revision scale of tests and in some cases by additional special tests; and second, detection of symptoms of aberrant nature commonly known as psychopathic, and including for our purpose both psychoneurotic and psychotic. Definite intelligence grades were established in 71 of the 82 cases. In 11 cases the intelligence grades were not settled for the reasons noted in the table.

The mental status of the group may be seen from the following tables:

1. TABLE SHOWING DIAGNOSIS OF INTELLIGENCE (I. Q.)
BASED ON THE STANFORD REVISION SCALE AND CLASSIFICATION

```
Intelligence  normal  ......(I. Q. 105-90)........ 9  (12.6%)
     "        dull normal...(I. Q.  89-80).......19  (26.7%)
     "        borderline ....(I. Q.  79-70)........20  (28.1%)
     "        feeble-minded.(I. Q.  69-50)........34  (32.3%)....71
     "        unclassified...(I. Q. not determined)............11
                                                              ——
                                                              82
```

```
Unclassified (because of)
    Tested by different scale .................2
    Tests inconclusive ......................8
         Psychotic ...................2
         Psychopathic ...............3
         Foreign language .......... 3
    Refused cooperation .....................1
                                             ——
                                             11
```

```
         Highest  I. Q.....................105
         Lowest   I. Q..................... 50
         Average  I. Q..................... 75
```

2. TABLE SHOWING DIAGNOSIS OF PSYCHIC DISORDERS

```
PSYCHOSES .................................................. 4
              Dementia præcox .................2
              Alcoholic psychoses ..............2

PSYCHOPATHIC CONDITIONS ................................... 4

EPILEPSIES ................................................ 3
                                                          ——
                                                          11
```

In this group the average intelligence is seen to be low (I. Q. 75), a mental age of 12 years, or a borderline grade. The reader should keep in mind the fact that the scale is based on measurement of unselected school children whose average grade is 100. The percentage of feeble-minded is seen to be strikingly high (32.3%), but since this is a selected group, it probably shows a higher proportion of defectives than a group of routine cases would. It may be noted in passing, however, that in a group of 91 girls of average age approximately 21 years examined by the same scale in 1916-17 at the New York State Reformatory for Women (Bedford), the percentage of feeble-minded was 29.1% ; borderline, 15.4% ; dull normal, 20% ; normal, 13.5%.

As for the mental disorders irrespective of the intelligence, 4 or 4.8% were actually insane and committable. Two of these were among the oldest of the group and were alcoholic habituates with delusions and deterioration. The other two were cases of dementia præcox, one afterwards committed to a state hospital, the other diagnosed at a state hospital and placed under the supervision of an agency.

Among the psychopathic disorders not actually insane and committable we have included only those whose make-up and reactions were so markedly characteristic that they could not escape this designation. Briefly described they were as follows: (1) Two emotionally unstable girls, one strongly antagonistic, paranoid, and secretive. Apparently she had fair intelligence, though it was impossible to grade her with certainty because of resistance to cooperation in tests. She had earned $10 at housework, and was intermittently efficient. She made a good appearance and said she had formerly taught school. Her erratic after-history will be touched on in the later study. (2) The other girl, of good home and family, had left school at the beginning of High because of a nervous breakdown. Later she studied music. At the time she came to our attention she was a telephone operator, having been in the same position five years. She was egotistical, flighty, sensitive, and highly emotional; developed convulsions during the birth of her child, and died. (3) A third was a psychopathic inferior, 22 years old, of dull normal intelligence, of very good family, but absolutely without ability to manage her-

13

self. She had had two illegitimate children by different men prior to the one with which our records are concerned. (4) The fourth, a refined English girl, was not graded by intelligence tests because of her emotional disturbance. She was out of touch with her mother and seemed quite alone in this country. Little history was obtainable. She was hysterical, secretive, and depressed. The epileptics were all of major type; two of the girls had been in a state hospital for epileptics; the third was feebleminded by test. Her father, she said, was also an epileptic. She had previously had two illegitimate children by different men.

From what we found by mental examination it was clear that there was no single or constant distinguishing feature to account for the experience. Ranging as they did from deeply feeble-minded to normal intelligence, from actual insanity through varying degrees of psychopathic instabilities and irregularities, to girls of relatively balanced commonsense, it was evident that there was no open-sesame either to the explanation of the problem or its management, but that each girl was a separate problem requiring individual study, interpretation, and treatment. When we could differentiate a psychotic entity, a pronounced psychopathic constitution or an actual intellectual defect, it gave a plausible and probably a cogent means of explaining the social shortcoming. It gave also a definite direction to the outlining of a program of management. But many girls did not fall into any of these relatively clear-cut categories. Yet even when they did not there was often a mental peculiarity, easy to see, but difficult to describe; a kind of friendly pliability towards the world, a tenderness toward themselves, a superficial fore-shortened outlook on life. Their emotional reaction was somehow inadequate to the situation. There was rarely any "righteous indignation" toward the defaulting partner, nor any censure of themselves, but rather a mild submissiveness as if they had little active responsibility in the matter—a pitying rather than a critical attitude.

B. SOME ITEMS OF THE PERSONAL HISTORY.

1. NATIONALITY

Of the total group (82) 56 were born in the United States, 9 in Ireland, 4 in the Maritime Province, 3 in Sweden, 2 in England, 1 each in Norway, Finland, and Germany. The birthplace of 5 was unknown.

2. AGE

The average age of the group is 21, the oldest 35, the youngest 14½ years.

```
There were  7 aged 14 to 16
           11   "   16 to 18
           43   "   18 to 25
           21   "    over 25
```

3. EDUCATION

```
Grammar  school  complete................ 8
More than grammar school................31
Less than  grammar  school................38
Illiterate  ............................. 2
Data uncertain  ....................,.... 3
                                        ──
                                        82
```

```
High  school  graduates.............5
Commercial  course ................3
State  Industrial  School...........2
```

More than grammar school means anything from a few months in high school or evening school to full graduation. No girl had more than a high school education.

AGE OF LEAVING SCHOOL

```
19  ............................... 1
18  ............................... 2
17  ............................... 8
16  ...............................10
15  ...............................12
14  ...............................16
13  ............................... 9
12  ............................... 1
11  ............................... 1
10  ............................... 0
 9  ............................... 1
Data  uncertain  .............21
                                ──
                                82
```

REASON FOR LEAVING SCHOOL (Girls' Statement)

```
To work ...........................39
Tired of school ......................13
      (fell behind and lost interest)
Pregnant  ........................... 7
Poor health ......................... 3
To help at home ..................... 7
"Persecution of teacher" ............. 1
Data  uncertain  .....................12
```

15

Lack of education as a contributory factor to motherhood without marriage is probably subsidiary to intellectual endowment. It will be noted that 5 of our girls had completed high school. Special vocational training would have been valuable to many who, because of limited intellectual endowment, found grade work irksome and left school to go to work in spite of our "14 year" law. Without adequate social supervision, under the strain of competition and criticism, and subjected to temptations they could not understand or withstand, they became easy sex victims of men and boys of their own type or even those of better intelligence who could not understand that minds are often much younger than bodies. The mental defectives, except for the foreign girls, could have been detected in the public schools if facilities for examination had existed. Fortunately, with the present provision for examination of retarded school children, we ought presently to see a diminution in the number of feeble-minded unmarried mothers, if the special training and the social supervision recommended by the school psychiatrists are carried out.

4. OCCUPATION

```
Not gainfully employed ...........................................10
      No occupation ......................................... 3
      Attending school ...................................... 6
      Housewives ........................................... 1
Professional persons ............................................. 0
Clerks and kindred workers ......................................14
      Bookkeepers, cashiers, stenographers, typewriters... 4
      Clerks (except clerks in stores) ...................... 2
      Clerks in stores and saleswomen ...................... 3
      Messenger, bundle and office girls ................... 1
      Telephone and telegraph operators ................... 4
Semiskilled workers .............................................30
      Dressmaker and seamstresses (not in factory)......... 2
      Laundry operatives .................................... 4
      Nurses (not trained) ................................. 0
      Semiskilled factory operatives .......................24
      Other ................................................ 0
Servants .......................................................28
      Charwomen, cleaners, laundresses .................... 1
      Waitresses ........................................... 4
      Domestic servants ...................................22
      Other (child governess) ............................. 1
Other ............................................................ 0
```
                                                              82

16

Comment on the occupations[1] of the subjects is omitted be
cause it is fully dealt with in the follow-up study.

5. LIVING PLACE AT TIME OF PREGNANCY

```
Own home ........................48
      Good ...................12
      Fair ...................23
      Poor ...................13
Boarding or lodging house........ 9
Working in families .............25
```

6. MARTIAL STATUS AT TIME OF PREGNANCY

```
Previously married (divorced 2; separated 2)...... 4
Unmarried ...........................................78
                                                    ───
                                                     82
```

7. NUMBER OF PRESENT PREGNANCY

```
First ...........................62
Second ......................17
Third ........................ 3
```

8. STATUS OF GIRLS' PARENTS AT TIME OF PREGNANCY

FATHER

```
Living ...........................................48
      Deserted ................................ 2
      Divorce or legal separation .............. 5
Dead .............................................22
Identity unknown (unmarried mother illeg.)...... 4
Data incomplete ................................ 8
                                                ───
                                                 82
```

MOTHER

```
Living ...........................................55
      Deserted ................................ 2
      Divorce or legal separation .............. 5
Dead .............................................19
Data incomplete ................................ 8
                                                ───
                                                 82
```

LOSS OF EITHER OR BOTH PARENTS BEFORE 13TH BIRTHDAY

	Of Father	Of Mother	Both
By death	12	10	1
By desertion	2	..	..
By divorce or legal separation	5	..	..
Surrender	..	1	1
Fact of being illegitimate....	4	2	2
	23	13	4

[1] Classification as used in "Illegitimacy as a Child-Welfare Problem", part 2, p. 122.

9.   BROTHERS AND SISTERS

None (only child) 8
1—12 68
Information uncertain 6

                                                 82

No history of delinquency 25
History of delinquency in 15
Information uncertain 42

                                                 82

C.   PHYSICAL EXAMINATION.

Systematic and complete physical examination was not at
the time our cases were under care (1914-18) a routine pro-
cedure with all of the agencies.   Records of findings were rarely
uniform or complete even when complete physical examination
had been made, therefore when reviewed yielded little of
diagnostic value.   The importance of the physical condition was
not overlooked, but it was considered more for its use in the
immediate management of the case than for its more general
scientific import.   Most of the agencies at that time were settling
the questions of syphilis and gonorrhea by having laboratory
tests made and were making practical use of the information, but
the results were not always definitely and accurately recorded.
At the time of the mental examination it was not often possible
or practicable to put the girl through a physical examination, but
an attempt was made in all cases to size up the general physical
condition: heart and lungs were examined and vision and hearing if defects were suspected.   Neurological examinations, more
or less complete, were frequently made.

Judging from such data as we have, we should say that the
physical make-up and health of the girls in this study average
up very well with that of other girls in similar social setting and
considerably better than a group of girls whose average age was
also 21 years, studied in a state reformatory, 1913-15.[1]   There
were a few cases of anemia and poor nutrition and some with

---

[1] "Physical State of Criminal Women", by Alberta S. B. Guibord,
M. D., *Journal of the American Institute of Criminal Law and Crimi-
nology*, Vol. 8, No. 1, May, 1917.

minor orthopedic defects, visual defects, naso-pharyngeal obstructions, poor teeth, etc., but there were also a few cases of excellent physical make-up and health. Seven girls had positive Wassermann, and several had positive gonorrhea tests; but since these records were not complete for the entire group the figures indicate the minimum only of venereal infection. Stigmata of degeneracy were present about as we meet them in a general population, and as far as we could see without any special relation to the mental status, except one feeble-minded subject (I. Q. 57) who had bilateral coloboma with marked visual defect.

We quote from the records made at the time of mental examination (April 5, 1917) for an illustration of one of the poorest physical specimens, a girl of 16 years who graded in the upper range of feeble-minded. "A pathetic half-starved looking girl * * pale, anemic, haggard, stoop shouldered, looks as if she had never had a square meal." Her father was alcoholic and deserted the mother who had to go to work to support five children in a poor slum district. Girl left school at 14 and went to work in a shoe factory to help support the family. Later she went to work in a plumber's shop at $5 a week and very shortly became pregnant by her employer, a man 45 years of age. The girl was barely able to stand when she left the hospital, but refused to remain there or to accept convalescent care. The outcome of this case will be specially noted in the follow-up. We also quote from the records to illustrate one of the best physical specimens. "A splendid physical make-up—without discoverable physical defect and in glowing health."

Whatever relation physical status may have to the incidence of pregnancy outside of marriage, through lessening inhibitions and initiative or through conducing to premature and uncontrolled sex expression, the discovery of it is not likely to be at or near the time of confinement when the whole physiological machinery is running in an exceptional way. The relation of physical condition to the social readjustment of the unmarried mother is of course very important. The agencies appear, for the most part, to take this into account and to provide for their girls the best possible condition of health before permitting them to go into the community.

19

D. FAMILY HISTORY.

In its bearing on the occurrence of motherhood without marriage family history obviously has the usual implications: (1) The hereditary aspect, in this case presumably a predisposition to irregular sex expression or perhaps other modes of antisocial behavior; (2) the environmental aspect, or the general setting of the home and the social and moral ideals and practices of the family.

In examining the records of the family history of the cases two defects were met: First, the failure to account for all members of a family; and second, the misleading custom in case-taking of recording pathological and adverse items, while omitting the normal and favorable ones. Some interesting facts appear in the family histories: of the girls in the study, 4 were themselves known to be illegitimate; 1 had a mother who was known to be illegitimate; 7 had sisters with at least one illegitimate child. Information is lacking as to how many fathers or brothers were of illegitimate birth, or how many fathers and brothers were themselves the fathers of illegitimate children. There occur frequently statements about various members of the families of "low grade mentality," "sex offender," "criminal record," etc. There are also some statements, not as many, of "intelligent," "self-respecting," etc. Much intensive investigation of family records is necessary before anything of the hereditary aspect of illegitimacy can be known. Without regard to its explanation, we note merely for its passing interest that in respect to bearing children out of wellock there is a slight evidence of similarity of reaction in sisters of our girls—whether more than a mere chance occurrence cannot be concluded from so small a number of cases. What has to be noted, however, as more than a coincidence, is the high proportion of "poor homes" and lack of wise parental guidance. Poor homes do not necessarily imply the lack of material things, though that too is frequent; but that the spirit of home is lacking—the atmosphere which makes a young person feel "at home" and contented in her own home, and at the same time endows her with good character and social and moral standards. A glance at our tables shows that

20

48, a trifle more than half, were living in their own homes at the time of the occurrence of pregnancy; of these 48 only 12 were reckoned as having good homes. Twenty-five were working as domestics in families, a situation which proverbially provides little "at home" feeling.

The foregoing sketchy presentation of the initial study obviously omits many important points germane to the incidence of unmarried motherhood such as religious influences, recreational facilities, sex education, and certain innate characteristics more particularly proclivity to sex expression. The relation of these various influences is not overlooked, but without more complete data than is at hand in our records it would be useless to introduce the subject at all. One conspicuous omission must be especially commented on, namely the partner, or the male factor involved in the unmarried motherhood experience. The importance of this aspect of the subject is self-evident. With 7 of the girls under 16 years of age, the statutory age of consent in Massachusetts, it is inevitable that the case records in this study should show a good deal of data regarding the partner. In fact it is just the preponderance of data that seems to make it impracticable to introduce the subject here. The material could be suitably presented only in a separate paper.

II. FOLLOW-UP STUDY

Introduction

It has already been indicated that Part II of this study will be devoted to a presentation of the facts obtained by following up at the expiration of a period varying from three to five years these 82 women whose mental status was determined by psychiatric examination, and who became illegitimately pregnant. A consideration of the social readjustment of the mother necessarily includes the fate of the child with whom her life is so inextricably woven.

For the purpose of this study the term "unmarried mother" will designate those who became pregnant without marriage, those who, although married, became pregnant by someone other than the husband, and those formerly married who had been divorced.

Scope and Method of Investigation

As Dr. Guibord has pointed out these were selected cases in as much as each presented some special problem which prompted the social agency to seek psychiatric advice as an aid in planning a satisfactory program for the future.

The social study is based upon analysis of the information obtainable from case records and from social workers who have known these mothers. In this way not only the agency which requested the mental examination but more than a dozen others located in four states have been called upon for assistance. Family, child-placing and medical agencies, maternity homes, probation and parole departments, public and private organizations alike, have shown an understanding of the purpose of the study and a splendid spirit of cooperation. The facts of history subsequent to agency care were secured by the organization responsible for the case at the time of mental examination or through its cooperation.

In collecting data only those sources were consulted which were known to have been cognizant of the fact of the illegitimate pregnancy. In this way the stories of these unmarried mothers have not been spread. No mother, child, or family has been injured by this study. While by this method it was in some instances impossible to secure all the facts which would have been helpful, it was considered fairest to all concerned.

Plan of Report Based On Two Theories of Care

Special emphasis is laid in this report on two points: First, the treatment given these mothers by social agencies because of its supposed influence on the outcome; second, the histories subsequent to care by the agencies. It is hoped by comparing outcome with original plans that some estimate of the merit of the methods used in dealing with the unmarried mother may result. .

Those who best know the problem are not in agreement as to the value of helping the mother to keep her child. On the one hand there are those who believe that the unmarried mother should do this; they feel that carrying the responsibility which a mother has for her offspring, legitimate or illegitimate, is her right and duty and should not be surrendered except for grave reasons; that the illegitimate child, like the legitimate, has a right to its natural mother's care and should not be deprived of a second parent because it has the misfortune to be born without a legal father. They rely upon the maternal instinct to develop and strengthen the mother's character. On the other hand there are those who hold that permanent separation serves the best interests of mother and child. They claim that adoption of the illegitimate child removes the stigma with which it is born and gives it an opportunity for such normal development as it could never have with its natural mother, while it allows the mother to live down her transgression free from its visible evidence. Miss Plows-Day in her "Reasons for Advocating Adoption for Illegitimate Children," says "the mother should be taught the necessity of renouncing and inspired to be willing to sacrifice her claim of motherhood, for the benefit of her child. * * * During my twenty years' work none of the mothers whom I have helped to be relieved of the burden of the support and complications which an illegitimate child entails has had a second or third, but all of those who have had second or third children have been those who were trying to support their illegitimate child, whether it was the

23

first, second or third."[1] Since any large amount of evidence to support the efficacy of either theory is lacking, what becomes of the unmarried mothers of this study has been considered in the light of whether they have kept the child or whether they have been permanently separated from it. An effort has been made to compare the mothers who have carried their responsibility with those who have surrendered or been relieved of it with a view to determining which mother makes the more successful social readjustment. Has the mother who has kept her child developed more strength of character, lost some of that "mild submissiveness" spoken of by Dr. Guibord and made a better recovery from her experience than the girl who has renounced "her claim of motherhood"? Have we put too much emphasis on keeping together or parting mother and child?

The phrase "kept the baby" is used in this report to mean the retention by the mother of the responsibility for the child. The responsibility may be moral or legal or both. Therefore the child kept by the mother may have remained with her continuously or have been placed away from her a part or all the time since birth. The point is there exists a present assumption of responsibility and a reasonable possibility of a further strengthening of the tie between mother and child.

The phrase "not kept the baby" is defined as permanent separation of mother and child such as is caused by death, legal surrender, or such circumstances as give no reasonable likelihood of the mother reassuming responsibility. Those mothers who from the first determined to be rid of the baby; those who preferred to keep it but were persuaded by agency, relatives, or friends to part with it; those who struggled to retain it but were forced to give it up by circumstances beyond their control; those who lost the baby by death; and the 2 mothers who died, 1 immediately after child birth, and 1 when the baby was 18 months old, are included here. Most cases clearly belong in one or the other classification, but there are some which demand

---

[1] Miss Plows-Day's "Reasons for Advocating Adoption for Illegitimate Children," placed before the Departmental Parliamentary Committee sitting to consider the subject of adoption with a view of formulating a bill legalizing it. London, December 5, 1920.

special mention. The most extreme example of "keeping the baby" under this definition is the following: A mother has contented herself with corresponding with the woman with whom she placed the child at board when a few weeks old and sending articles of clothing. She has never visited, but forces the child's father to pay the board. She has made no effort to have the child adopted or to shift the care to an agency. Her inclusion in this class hinges on the fact that though her interest is largely negative, this mother recognizes a responsibility. On the other hand, 2 mothers placed the child with a public agency expecting to reassume the care at some future time. Their mental condition is such that the probability of their carrying their own burden is very remote. These mothers are considered as separated from the child.

DIVISION INTO GROUPS I, II, AND III

For purposes of study on the lines indicated the 82 mothers have been placed in three groups: Group I, composed of those who have kept the baby; Group II, of those who have been separated from it; and Group III, made up of those mothers whose disappearance with the child has made it impossible to determine whether they have kept it. Comparison of these groups shows several things: First, 41 mothers—exactly half the total number—are known to have kept the child; 34 including 2 mothers who have died, to have been separated from it; 7 mothers to have disappeared with it. Second, two-thirds of all those of normal intelligence and nearly three-fourths of those of dull normal intelligence kept the child; so also did approximately half the feeble-minded and the borderline. The 3 mothers with epilepsy, the 2 with dementia præcox, and 3 of the 4 psychoneurotics are in Group II. All of Group III are below dull normal, 4 of them feeble-minded. Third, about two-thirds of the girls whose education was the equivalent of more than grammar school are in Group I, and also slightly more than one-half of those whose education was the equivalent of less than grammar school. No member of Group III had as much as grammar school education. For 62, about three-fourths of all the mothers in this study, this was probably the first illegitimate pregnancy.   Nearly one-half of these are known to have kept the child.

HISTORY PRIOR TO TREATMENT

Family.   The material at hand concerning the family histories of these 82 mothers but adds to the data dealt with in the studies previously mentioned.   The more one knows concerning the stock from which these girls came and the conditions under which they lived, the easier it is to understand how they became unmarried mothers.

As treatment is considered, the facts of family history should be borne in mind as showing with what sort of human material the agencies had to deal.   Only 8 girls became pregnant while living in their own home in which both parents were living and maintaining standards of self-support and decency and providing reasonable opportunities for the normal development of their children.   One is struck by the fact that so many were living away from home—almost half of the whole number—until one looks for explanation.   Many of these homes were broken by the death of one or both parents, by divorce or separation, by desertion, or were made abnormal by alcohol, immorality, non-support, defective intelligence, mental or physical disease.   Four of these young mothers were themselves illegitimate; 2 of them had been kept by their respective mothers; each of these girls in turn kept her child.   In the other 2 cases one mother was brought up by relatives from birth, and the other was twice adopted and completely lost her real identity.   Numerous other instances exist of irregular sex conduct on the part of parents and siblings of these girls.   On this point Dr. Kammerer says, "It is probable that among the most contaminating of all experiences which a young girl may go through short of actual physical intercourse is that produced by the knowledge and sight of paternal immorality."[1]

Occupational.   The majority of these mothers were poorly equipped for industrial life.   This is not surprising when it is considered that the average intelligence quotient was below 75, that

---

[1] Kammerer, Percy Gamble: "The Unmarried Mother," Boston, 1918.

nearly five-eighths of all had education equivalent to or less than grammar school, and that approximately 1 girl in 3 left school by the time she was 14 years old. The result was that many entered unskilled employment at low pay and shifted frequently from one job to another. For this reason care should be taken not to attach too much significance to the fact that the mother was engaged in this or that occupation at the time of application to the agency. Of more importance is the actual economic status. An attempt has been made to determine this by considering the occupational history of each mother.

Much of the data available is incomplete in that it lacks such facts as a full list of positions held, the particular employment within the industry, the wage earned and the time spent in each job. The following comment from "Illegitimacy as a Child-Welfare Problem" shows that the same difficulties were encountered and recognized in securing information for that great study. "It is evident that the information here given is only a rough approximation of economic status, because of the failure of the records in most cases to report specific employments within the industries and the wages earned."[1]

At the time of application to the agency approximately 7 of every 10 mothers were employed as "semiskilled workers" or as "servants," about an equal number in each class. Considerably less than one-fifth were working as "clerk or kindred workers" while one-eighth were not gainfully employed. One-third of those at work had changed not only jobs, but type of employment. For example, one girl of borderline intelligence, industrious but untrained in any particular work held five positions previous to confinement, two at housework, two as factory operative, and one in a laundry. She had, therefore, changed from the "semiskilled workers" to the "servant"[2] class and back again. More than one-third the total number of mothers had had some experience in housework outside their own home.

[1] Children's Bureau: "Illegitimacy as a Child-Welfare Problem," part 2, Washington, 1921.
[2] This classification is that used by the Children's Bureau in "Illegitimacy as a Child-Welfare Problem," part 2, p. 122.

SECTION 1

TREATMENT

PSYCHIATRIST'S EXAMINATION AND RECOMMENDATION

It has already been pointed out that "the mental examination was sought by the agencies as a diagnostic aid in helping to understand the girl for the purpose of making a satisfactory program for her future." It is important to stress the point that such an examination is not merely for the purpose of discovering defects; it also detects special mental ability and is of service in vocational guidance. In the case of the mothers under consideration the mental examination resulted not only in grading them according to intelligence and discovering traces of mental disorder irrespective of intelligence but it brought about specific recommendations regarding approximately one-half the total number. These indicated that certain girls should be given custodial care; that others though of low grade or defective intelligence could be cared for in the community under close supervision; that a few needed observation in an institution for further study of their mental condition; that some were of sufficient intelligence to be able to take advantage of further education; that this mother should be given housework, and that, an employment requiring more skill. That is to say the suggestions were definite and constructive, aiming at the protection of the mothers and of the community and seeking to have each mother perform the highest form of work of which she was capable. The recommendations related to 14 of the 41 mothers of Group I. The social agencies planned their treatment at least for a time according to psychiatric advice in 6 of these cases. The result was that special emphasis was laid on the kind of work given 2 mothers, an attempt to furnish close supervision for 2 others, and an earnest although unsuccessful effort to secure institutional custody for 2 of the 6 feeble-minded of this Group for whom such care was urged. In one of these cases the agency which had had supervision of the mother from the time she was a child tried repeatedly to obtain custodial care for her. It was not until her conduct had brought her before the court that the mother was committed, and then it was to a penal institution instead of to a school for the mentally defective and after she was illegitimately pregnant. In the other case, while the social agency was in correspondence with the school for the feeble-minded, the girl's marriage to a man many years her senior was brought about by her mother.

The following are some of the instances in which the recommendations of the psychiatrist were not followed: A mother of normal intelligence who had had experience in clerical work as well as in housework was placed at domestic service without her child, although the psychiatrist advised "something more congenial and skilled than housework." A mother, low grade feeble-minded, belonging in another state but brought here for confinement, was placed in a public institution after her return to her home state; in spite of the recommendation that she be given permanent institutional care, she was placed at housework with her child after some months and later at the same work without the child. A mother was placed at housework with her child after it had been recommended by the psychiatrist that she be given more education to enable her to take a higher grade position. Another mother suffering from an alcoholic psychosis withdrew her application for help in caring for her child, and therefore it was not possible for lack of legal control to provide supervision; accordingly, she returned to the community with this her second illegitimate child to give birth later to her third.

Definite recommendations following mental examination were made to the agencies regarding 15 mothers of Group II. In 8 instances the advice was followed, resulting in concrete plans in several cases such as permanent custodial care of 2 mothers, 1 feeble-minded and 1 insane; institutional care with periods of parole for 2 epileptics; placing in the care of the United States Immigration Authorities for deportation of 1 feeble-minded; supervision in the community under the care of a hospital of 1 suffering from dementia præcox; and careful placing in a foster home of a young mother who needed wholesome contacts and the right job to offset the effects of her former home life. On the other hand 2 mothers were not returned to the psychiatrist for completion of the examination, and are therefore unclassified in this report; another mother for whom custodial care or close supervision was recommended has disappeared, leaving her child dependent upon public care; another for whom custodial care was urged at least during child-bearing period remains in the community unsupervised, having married after giving birth to two illegitimate children. In still another out-of-state case special care in placing was suggested: "Because girl has never had a chance, place for one or two years under good hygienic and nutritive conditions and then re-test." At the end of one year of inferior placing this mother, then 15 years old, with an intelligence quotient of 57 was placed in an industrial school where she remained for nearly three years when she was again placed at housework. The supervision needed by 2 other mothers was not provided.

Specific recommendations were made in the cases of 3 of the mothers of Group III. In one case the advice was followed resulting in the deportation of a feeble-minded mother and her child. In another case the mother graded as of feeble-minded intelligence was sent to a public institution for treatment of venereal disease. The psychiatrist recommended observation while there to determine the mental condition. There is no record at the institution of any request for observation and none was made. The third mother who had deserted her husband and three legitimate children was suffering from alcoholic psychosis. Her condition was such that commitment was desirable. She disappeared on her way to the almshouse.

These facts show that of every two recommendations made as a result of the mental examination the social agencies attempted to follow one. Even allowing for the burden of current cases carried by practically every case worker which causes actual accomplishment to fall short of desire, and for the fact that but 4 of these mothers were in the legal control of an agency enabling it to force treatment, it seems fair to conclude that the significance of the mental examination was not fully understood or the recommendations of the psychiatrist would have been followed in a larger number of cases. It must, however, be remembered in fairness to the social agencies that adequate care of the feeble-minded in Massachusetts is not yet provided. Although the outlook is hopeful in that a sufficient appropriation has been secured to carry out the plan of the State Department of Mental Diseases "for a division within the Department to handle the problem of the feeble-minded; in particular to organize more fully the extramural supervision and service which has been growing so rapidly in Massachusetts,"[1] the present facilities for housing those in need of custodial care are insufficient; centralized authoritative supervision of all those who could be cared for in the community with safety to themselves and others does not exist. Under these conditions failure to secure adequate care for most of the feeble-minded girls of this study is not so much to be wondered at as the lack of concerted effort to bring about proper supervision for the mentally defective of the State. In 1914 a registry of the feeble-minded was undertaken and maintained by the League for Preventive Work in Boston. It was hoped that an approximately complete list of the feeble-minded coming to the attention of the social agencies of the State would be secured and later turned over to a public department as an aid in working out a scheme of institutional and extramural care. The discouragement of the social agencies in being unable to secure proper care for the feeble-minded with whom they deal is at least a partial explanation of the fact that but 8 of the 23 feeble-minded mothers of this study were registered with the League for Preventive Work.

It is obvious that no general policy of helping the mother to keep the child or aiding her to become permanently separated from it was based on her intelligence as it has already been indicated that some mothers of each grade of intelligence kept the child.

AGENCY PLACEMENT

It is to the credit of the agencies that ample time for convalescence and regaining of strength was allowed the mother following the birth of the child. When social treatment began, the organizations resorted most frequently to one of two methods in

---

[1] *Bulletin,* Boston Council of Social Agencies, April, 1922.

31

dealing with the mother: First, returning her with the child to her relatives, whenever wise and possible; second, placing her at work with the child. Although these mothers are now found distributed among the three Groups, it is significant that in only 6 cases did a social agency make its first plan with the idea of helping the mother give up the child. Often the first arrangement was shortlived, as in the case of a low grade feeble-minded mother who was placed at housework with her child and after a few days was found to be so incapable of either housework or care of the child that she was committed to a school for the feeble-minded. Frequently the first plan was experimental and was tried in the hope of persuading, training, or something almost compelling the mother to keep the child. The point is that the agencies tried to find some way of keeping mother and child together and made other disposition only when this failed.

With Relatives. As the placements show, the mother's reestablishment was begun whenever possible by making her again a member of her own family group.

In Group I there are 3 babies who were born at the home of their maternal grandparents. Ten mothers returned to their parents' home upon discharge from the place of confinement; 2 went to other relatives. In other words, 15 mothers were actually living with relatives at or soon after the birth of the child and all but 1 had the child with her. In 12 instances the mother's return to her family came about later; 7 took the baby home, 5 placed it at board.

Two mothers of Group II were confined at home; 7, 4 with the baby, went directly home from the place of confinement; another, without the child, went at once to relatives; 5 others, 1 with the baby, found their way home after a considerable period of time. In addition there were 3 mothers who, without the child, went to some family connection at the end of a few months.

No mother of Group III went directly to relatives after confinement although 3 are known to have gone later, 2 with the child. Two of these out-of-state girls were placed by the agencies with the child at the State Infirmary. They were then turned over to the authorities of their respective states, and finally discharged to relatives. The third mother boarded the child and went to live with her sister after a period at housework with the baby. It is probable that still another mother who was deported with the child eventually found her way home.

Forty-eight, or more than one-half the total number of mothers, 30 of them with the child, were finally in the home of some relative. This is inclusive of the 5 mothers who gave birth to the child at her parents' home.

In Employment. For mothers who did not go directly home from the place of confinement, for those who came into agency care after the baby born at home had been given away by the family, for those who had reached a crisis in their struggle to keep the child, and for those mothers whom it was impossible or unwise to return to relatives, the agencies made further provision. Employment was the most conspicuous need of the largest number. It appears that work was found for 18 of the mothers of Group I, 16 at housework and 2 at wet nursing. Fifteen of these had the baby with her at the place of employment. Fifteen of Group II were placed at work; 14 at housework, 1 as a wet nurse. In 11 instances the girl was placed with the baby. Employment was found for 2 of Group III. Both were placed at housework with the child.

Domestic service and wet nursing were the only kinds of work provided as a first job by the agencies. Regardless of intelligence, occupational experience or training, all but the 3 mothers placed as wet nurses were given a trial at housework.

The advantages of an occupation which provides a family home where a mother may have the actual care of the child with an opportunity to nurse it and at the same time earn a wage over and above her board are easily seen. Moreover, the constant, kindly oversight and training in right standards of living as well as of work which an intelligent and sympathetic housewife can give, especially to a young girl, is of inestimable help to her. The cooperation of the carefully selected employer or foster mother is invaluable to the social worker responsible for supervision. The selection of family homes capable of doing this constructive job with the mother and at the same time providing suitable occupation is a difficult task and requires the expert skill of a social worker trained in placing-out methods. Otherwise the

33

placing is too often not the adjusting of a particular girl to a particular family, but the haphazard putting of a girl who needs a job with a family seeking cheap help. The placements made of these mothers show all the grades of effort from unskilled job-finding by agencies unequipped for this specialty to the excellent painstaking work of placing-out societies. The good or ill which may result from placing in a family home is very great. When one considers the unfortunate and often serious consequences of improper placing, one is forced to question whether it is not better for the agency unequipped to do this specialized job well, to omit from its program of treatment all attempt to employ foster home care.

It is possible that unskillful placing may have been somewhat responsible for the evident unpopularity of housework as shown by the fact that at the end of one month after placement 4 mothers had left housework, 2 placed with the child and 2 placed alone. At the end of three months, 4 more girls had ceased to do this work, 3 placed with, and 1 without the child. So that at the end of three months one-fourth of the 32 placed at housework had given up this employment. Three months later the number leaving had increased to 13 of whom 8 belong to Group I.

The fact that one-fourth the total number placed had left the employment provided by the agencies at the end of three months and about two-fifths at the end of six months raises the question of the wisdom of the original plan especially in view of the fact that not all mothers placed with the child were nursing it. At the expiration of the first year after placement 12 mothers remainded at housework with the child, 8 of Group I, 2 of each of the other two groups. Seven of these are above the border-line grade of intelligence, but 1 is feeble-minded. Only 1 mother placed by an agency continued at domestic service as long as twenty months.

For Training. The agencies provided special training for a total of 5 mothers, 2 of Group I, 3 of Group II. In Group I a promising girl of normal intelligence was given three months in an excellent school of dressmaking. The course was completed creditably. The plan of having her earn a living for

34

herself and child as a dressmaker failed because of further sex irregularity. Therefore even after special opportunity was given and ability for dressmaking shown, she was again placed at housework with the child in order that she should receive supervision throughout the twenty-four hours. The other mother of this Group for whom further education was planned was a little girl just over 14 at the birth of her baby. Arrangements were made for her to attend continuation school but they were not carried out because of lack of cooperation on the part of her parents to whom she returned.

Three mothers of Group II were given special training, 2 of these were placed at housework. They came from homes of low house-keeping standards. In each case it was a child-placing agency which used the carefully selected foster family to educate the mother in those fundamentals of domestic work which she should have learned in her own home. In this way the mother who had the baby with her through this period was also taught to care for her own child; the second mother had been separated from her child before becoming known to the agency. Opportunity was later given to train for a child's attendant. The third mother was sent to business school to complete a stenographic course begun in high school.

From the foregoing it is evident that not much was done to give further education or special training to these mothers in spite of the fact that nearly half of the entire number had less than grammar school education and that a very small proportion had what could be considered training for earning a living. Dr. Guibord has pointed out that trade school and special vocational training would have been valuable to a considerable number of those of limited intelligence.

After a period at housework varying as already stated from three months to more than a year the agencies next helped or allowed all but one of those mothers remaining in care to undertake different employment which necessitated boarding the child. In a few cases it was still possible to have mother and child in the same family home. The range of employment entered into is shown by the following illustrations: ward maid in a hospital, laundress in the maternity home where she had been confined and where as an employee she was given supervision, factory worker who returned to the child at night, cook at $12.00 per week.

The case of one mother who has been in the care of a public agency for some ten years is interesting as illustrating the wisdom of sometimes allowing a girl to choose her own occupation. This mother of dull normal intelligence was kept at housework for years before pregnancy. She was difficult to place because she did not get on well with children. She disliked housework and was a failure in it. In three years and seven months she had been in fourteen homes; yet she managed to earn her board, an opportunity to attend school and sometimes wages of $1.00 per week. After confinement this mother, previously unable to deal successfully with children, surprised those who knew her best by her determination to keep the baby. For three months she worked at domestic service with it. Then the wise and understanding visitor whose policy has always been to give the girl all the responsibility that she could carry without being crushed by it permitted her to choose her own work. After one or two unsatisfactory short time jobs the mother found employment in a shoe factory and earned from $15.00 to $19.20 a week. She supported herself and child almost entirely until marriage and was anxious to shoulder her own burden. The visitor has had the deep satisfaction which comes from watching an unpromising child develop into a worthwhile wife and mother. Unquestionably the self-respect and sense of responsibility engendered by being allowed freedom to leave the occupation which she disliked and to select her own method of earning a living played an important part in this girl's development.

Other Services. In a few cases the social agencies rendered services in addition to those already enumerated, such as boarding mother and child together pending a final plan. For example: A mother and baby were boarded together until marriage to the father; another until the child was taken for permanent care by its father; others until the mothers could return to relatives and the child be placed at board. Apparently only 3 mothers have been able to manage their own affairs without further assistance from agency or relatives since discharged from the place of confinement.

But 4 marriages of Group I were brought about or aided by social agencies. One of these occurred before the child's birth. In this instance the mother realized that marriage to the father would probably not bring happiness; yet she felt she ought to secure a name for her child and so followed the counsel of the agency. She and her husband have separated. She is said to be satisfied that the sacrifice for the child's sake was worth while. Another mother remained at housework with the baby until marriage to the father of the child seventeen months after its birth. The man had returned from war penitent and had turned to the agency which had cared for the girl for help in finding her. A happy marriage has resulted. The third mother was married to the father of the child three years after its birth. Careful study of the mother, various attempts to provide her with suitable occupation, and close supervision had failed to prevent further sex irregularity in spite of her love for the baby. The marriage which she and the child's father desired was finally allowed. As far as can be ascertained this mother has remained true to her husband.[1] In the case of the fourth marriage the mother, unclassified as to intelligence but said by the psychiatrist not to be feeble-minded, became pregnant by and married a man not the father of her child of 20 months while she was at housework with the baby and receiving really excellent care under the supervision of an agency. Since marriage she has settled down to a normal life. A fifth mother, graded as dull normal, was married while pregnant to the father of her child and without the knowledge of the agency, immediately before her acceptance for care by a maternity home.

There is but 1 marriage in Group II for which an agency was in any way responsible. In this case a place was secured for mother and child to board together until the marriage to the father of the child took place when it was 6 weeks old.

No marriages in Group III were brought about through agency activity.

---

[1] As this report goes to press the mother was convicted of adultery and cross libels for divorce have been filed.

Of the 82 mothers under consideration 61, 18 years or over, were unmarried or divorced and therefore free to marry. A total of 5 marriages can be credited to the agencies, 1 girl being under 18 years of age. In respect to intelligence, 2 mothers were normal, 1 dull normal, 1 borderline, and 1 unclassified. This would seem to indicate that the social agencies here represented do not regard marriage even to legitimatize a child as the one great solution of the problem; rather do they seem to discourage it unless there is some reasonable expectation of permanency and happiness in the relationship which will make for a suitable environment for the child.

Separation of Mother and Child

Death. Death of the baby occurred in only 3 cases while the mother and child were in the care of the agency, a favorable commentary on agency care. One baby died suddenly when a few weeks old; another, a twin, at 3 months; the third was 5 months and had never been well. There was one stillbirth.

Agency responsibility

Adoption.—The agencies had a major responsibility in allowing 12 mothers to part with the child. Of this number 5 were adopted, 1 given to its father, 6 placed in public care. This means that about one-third the total number of separations which occurred were due to the influence of agencies. Two of the adoptions were arranged when the baby was under 6 months, 1 when about 1 year of age, 2 when 4 and 6 years, respectively. The social grade of the mother who came from and returned to a comfortable home, together with a determination on her part and that of her family to rid themselves of the child seem to be the reasons for the agency's decision in placing 1 of the 2 young babies; the apparent incompetency of a foreign-born mother and the wishes of her relatives the reasons in the other. Apart from the question of separation, whether the adoption of these 2 children whose mothers were designated by the psychiatrist as "unclassified" was a wise plan is another matter. In the case of the year old child, the agency stood aside and allowed the mother of borderline intelligence to

38

make her own decision as to whether it should be adopted by the foster mother. Every effort was made by an excellent child-placing agency to develop and equip the mothers of the 2 older children to care properly for them. Further education was given one, intensive training in housework and care of her baby, the other. Each was tried with and without the child. Finally it was decided that only permanent separation could assure either child a fair chance. It is to be noted that the intelligence of both these mothers was determined before adoption was decided upon. One was found to grade normal, the other dull normal. Both children have been studied from birth, both are on trial for adoption with people who have been carefully investigated to determine whether they have the character, fitness, and material resources to become suitable adoptive parents. If all is satisfactory at the end of a sufficiently long period, which will probably be not less than one year, to demonstrate that the particular child fits into the particular family, adoption papers will be presented to the court for signature. Surely such safeguards are preferable to any hastily determined methods of transplanting a human life. These agencies considered adoption a serious matter. This is further illustrated by a case in which an agency deliberately brought about the annulment of an unwise adoption for which it was in no way responsible.

Giving Child to Relatives.—One young mother was persuaded to give her child to its father who married the mother's maternal aunt. Unfortunately it has not yet been legally adopted so that it is still illegitimate and without proven claim on its father. This is one of several cases in which further pressure on the part of an agency might have brought about better legal status for the child.

Public Care.—The agencies have been instrumental in securing public care for 6 children. The mother's mental condition was the reason in each case. Two were committed to an institution, one a hospital for the insane, the other a school for the feeble-minded; 2 were epileptic and sent to a hospital, but as voluntary patients who could not be committed because their condition was not "dangerous to the public." They have been, therefore, in and out of the institution. The child of one of the epileptic mothers was born there following a period of parole in the community and placed within a few days of birth with the public authorities. The child of the other epileptic mother was cared for by a private agency until over 3 years of age then transferred to a public department. Two other mothers, both low grade feeble-minded, were persuaded to place the child in public care.

SUPERVISION

The supervision given by the agencies varied in length of time, quality of service, and value. In a few cases it was merely contact between agency and mother during investigation as in the case of the woman suffering from an alcoholic psychosis whose withdrawal of her appeal for help and subsequent handling of her own problem deprived the agency of any opportunity for supervision. In others it was carefully thought-out oversight continuing over a period of years and based on sympathetic understanding of the girl—a constant effort to energize her to continue safely alone.

It has been difficult to determine the exact duration of supervision because in so few instances is a definite date given on which the case became inactive and the agency surrendered responsibility. Instead there has been an apparent dwindling of interest as contact between mother and agency grew more infrequent and finally ceased. In other cases there was an apparent activity and responsibility on the agency's part which ended abruptly. In other instances a friendly, unofficial relationship has been maintained between one of the agency's staff and the mother. But 5 mothers have been given continuous supervision from the birth of the child, 2 by the agency responsible at the time of confinement, 2 in institutions, 1 who was transferred from the first agency to the second and remains under the care of the latter. Four of these are under legal control. In addition there are 3 mothers formerly in agency care who receive considerable advice and oversight because of the child still in charge of the organization. The nature of the unmarried mother's difficulty naturally prompts her to break loose as soon as possible from the contacts made at the time of confinement. Frequently

the girl who most needs guidance is the most resentful of it. It
is the mother's privilege to make supervision impossible unless
there is legal control to compel it. Too often with the cessation
of oversight comes unsuitable care for the child. This is the
opportunity for the mother who is bound to be rid of her child
to dispose of it. For the mother who would like to keep the
child but finds the struggle too difficult, it is the time of tempta-
tion. It is easy to find people eager to adopt. She finds the
argument that the child will have more than she can give so con-
vincing. Four of these mothers placed the child for adoption
almost as soon as supervision ended. Two more discouraged by
the outlook of the future placed the child with the idea of adoption and later were most thankful to receive it again. In one
instance this came about because the prospective adoptive parents
decided that the baby did not sufficiently resemble them; in the
other case a placing-out agency by boarding the child for a few
months and meanwhile adjusting the young mother's family difficulties made it possible for her to keep the child.

Consideration of the oversight given the mothers of this
study shows that while the object was to see each girl through at
least to the point where she had a reasonable chance to recover
socially from her experience, the pressure of current cases de-
manding the full strength of the staff, the frequent desire of the
mother to go her own way as soon as she recovered physically,
and the lack of legal control combined to make it impossible for
the agencies to follow the majority as closely or as long as desirable. Evidence exists in these 82 cases to demonstrate that
proper care for the child was many times dependent upon supervision. The subsequent history (page 60), will show that society
in one way or another through its courts, penal institutions, relief,
health, and other agencies has already been called upon to give
further supervision and help to some of these same mothers who
are unable to manage their own life without assistance. Obviously to follow indefinitely every woman who gives birth to an
illegitimate child would be absurd. In the light of what is already known may it not be well to consider whether the fate of
these already handicapped children should continue to rest so
largely with the mother? The Children's Bureau of the Depart-

ment of Labor held in 1920 two regional conferences on standards of legal protection for children born out of wedlock. The conclusions may be summarized briefly as follows: " * * * The parents should not be permitted to surrender a child for adoption, or to transfer guardianship, or to place it out permanently for care, without order of the court or state department made after investigation."[1] Minnesota in its law of 1920 took the position that it is the State's business to be responsible for the illegitimate child's welfare and through its State Board of Control assumed supervision of all illegitimate children up to 16 years of age or until some satisfactory disposition is made of the child. The power to dispose of the illegitimate child is taken from those who may be unable or unwilling to secure proper care for it.

ANALYSIS OF TREATMENT

Analysis of the treatment given these 82 mothers by the social agencies shows: (1) That the underlying theory was adaptation of care to individual need; (2) that nevertheless in many cases individual treatment did not go far enough; it stopped short of seeing the mother through to the point where she was able to proceed alone with safety to herself and the community or, when incapable of managing her life, to the point of securing adequate protection and supervision and (3) that failure to regard each unmarried mother as an integral part of a great social problem as well as an individual resulted in further suffering in so far as it postponed the laying of a foundation of constructive policies.

The seeking of a mental examination of each girl is an indication that an attempt was made to understand the individual presumably for the purpose of meeting her needs. On the other hand the agencies seem to have lost sight of individual needs in making their first plan—in all but 6 cases—with the idea of helping the mother to keep the child. The attempt to individualize treatment and at the same time to make it conform to this policy resulted frequently in fruitless work.

---

[1] Lenroot, Katharine F.: "Social Responsibility for the Protection of Children Handicapped by Illegitimate Birth." The Annals of the American Academy of Political and Social Science, November, 1921.

The psychiatric examination showed that the mental equipment of these mothers varied from normal to feeble-minded, from emotional stability to extreme instability, and thereby indicated that the range of accomplishment which could reasonably be expected differed considerably. The recommendations made by the psychiatrist aimed to develop each mother to capacity, or to protect her by custodial care within or without an institution when the best interest of the individual and the community demanded it. Consistent emphasis on the adaptation of care to individual needs would have resulted in an attempt to give each the advantage of the treatment prescribed or indicated as being within the grasp of her intelligence.

The agencies attempted to follow about half the recommendations based on the psychiatric examination. It is evident, therefore, that some mothers were not given treatment prescribed by the psychiatrist as beneficial to the individual. On the other hand it is encouraging to find social agencies beginning to utilize the scientific findings concerning the mental equipment of the individual as they use the facts bearing on the physical. While the recommendations followed were too few to warrant sweeping conclusions as to the practical value of the psychiatric examination in treatment, the results were such in certain cases as to make further trial highly desirable. It is reasonable to expect that with full appreciation of the significance of the psychiatrist's findings will come the adapting of the load to the mental as well as the physical carrying capacity of the bearer. It will tend to prevent the mother whose intelligence shows her incapable of successful management of her own life being encouraged to assume the guidance of her child's upbringing, and with the termination of supervision being left to do the job as best she can.

To claim that the social worker's "mere commonsense and background of experience provide as good a working instrument as the psychiatric examination in devising an effective program for the girl" is as unreasonable as to hold that commonsense and experience make a physical examination unnecessary.

In too many cases in spite of the beginning made towards individualizing treatment, the mother, with confinement over and health restored, became but one of a group of unmarried mothers indiscriminately encouraged to keep the child. As a result the question frequently became "by what means can the mother keep the child?" rather than "in planning for the future what is best for this mother, this child, and society?"

This change of emphasis in treatment appears again in a lack of individualization in providing employment. One of two kinds of work, domestic service and wet nursing, both calculated to keep mother and child together, was provided as a first job by the agencies. While the advantages of breast feeding and of good family home care are recognized, it is improbable that adaptation of treatment to individual need was the compelling reason for placing 25 of the 29 mothers for whom employment was provided by the agencies, at housework. Indeed, the psychiatric examination had definitely suggested care better suited to the development and protection of certain mothers.

Insufficient funds, pressure of the current case load, desire on the part of the mother to be free from supervision, lack of the agency's legal right to compel submission to treatment, and inadequate provision for the feeble-minded were additional factors resulting in termination of care in too many instances without fulfilling the real need of the individual.

The most advanced social agencies frankly recognize their inability to carry treatment in many cases far enough and for a sufficiently long time to insure proper readjustment or protection for the individual. They therefore see the wisdom of concerted action in attacking a large problem like feeble-mindedness.

These same agencies are aware of the inter-relation of feeble-mindedness and illegitimacy and believe public control of the feeble-minded necessary as a means of preventing and effectively dealing with the unmarried mother. Yet the chance to pool information by registering their feeble-minded women and thus to help convince the legislature of the shortsightedness of society in withholding protection for the mentally defective unmarried mother was overlooked in two-thirds of the cases of the feeble-minded of the study. (See p. 31.) The persistency of the habit of regarding illegitimacy as the concern alone of the unfortunate individual and her family was probably largely responsible for failure to see each unmarried mother as an integral part of a

44

great social problem. In addition to the kindly, patient, sincere interest and good case work which characterizes much of the work done with the illegitimately pregnant girl there must be the ability to see the individual and the problem in their interrelation. Only by thoroughgoing case work with as many unmarried mothers as the time of agencies permits and by study of many related cases, can a basis for safe generalizations be made which will in the truest sense help the individual.

SECTION 2

SUBSEQUENT HISTORY

In subsequent history it is intended to include the life of these mothers from the time the social agency ended care to approximately August 1, 1921. This period varies in length according to the time the agency supervised. It has already been noted that some supervision is still being given 5 mothers while contact is maintained with others. The majority for a considerable time have been living free from agency influence.

MENTAL CONDITION

Only another examination could give the present mental condition of those mothers who were suffering from some psychic disorder when seen by the psychiatrist. However, information secured as to how they are conducting themselves may throw some light on the subject. The one mother of Group I classified as psychoneurotic is at home with the child of whom she is fond, both supported by her father. To the lay mind there is nothing noteworthy in her conduct.

Nine of the 11 with some kind of psychic disorder are in Group II. Of the dementia præcox patients one committed following confinement remains at the hospital, the other in the community but under informal supervision delegated to a family agency by the hospital which gave a short period of observation. This mother married after giving birth to and placing for adoption two illegitimate children. She is now managing acceptably a comfortable home for her legitimate child and husband, a Japanese. The 2 epileptics who as voluntary patients were admitted two and three times respectively to a hospital are in the community without supervision of any kind. One escaped from the institution and is living in an adjoining state. It has not been possible to obtain information regarding her mental condition. The other was released three times to relatives who took no further responsibility and for months at a time have not known her whereabouts. A physician who has treated her claims to

46

have prevented all seizures during approximately the last two years. Another mother, of feeble-minded intelligence and probably epileptic, seemed at one time to be deteriorating, but for more than a year has occupied the position of attendant at a state hospital. The victim of alcoholic psychosis is the only one of this Group able to support herself and child without aid from relatives or agency.

Of the 3 psychoneurotics, one died following childbirth; another married and has a legitimate child. She is one of the steadiest workers of all the mothers under consideration, having held her first position in a department store more than six years, yet she has been one of the most difficult to follow up, seeming to show the same emotional resistance to cooperate in this as in the mental examination. The third has shown herself efficient in domestic service. She is able to obtain good positions and has earned as much as $12.00 per week. She contributed towards the support of her second illegitimate child whom she had by a colored man until recently, when she disappeared leaving the child at board.

Information is lacking regarding the alcoholic psychotic of Group III.

DIFFICULTIES ENCOUNTERED BY MOTHER IN KEEPING CHILD

It should be borne in mind that keeping the child is in most cases an heroic undertaking for an unmarried mother. For some of these under consideration it has meant tremendous sacrifice. Relatives who have stood by one girl, given her a home, and helped with, but not received the child, tell of the mother's constant worry and brave struggle to support it. They see nothing ahead for this proud, self-respecting young woman but more worry and sacrifice unless she parts with the child to whom she is devoted. Another mother already referred to carries her secret, sharing it only with her parents. To tell means disgrace in a community where she and her family are respected; to continue to live as she has for the past four years means unending strain to support and haunting fear lest the truth be discovered. "The woman from * * * * said she would help me but she wants to take my A—— away after my hard time trying my best to keep her and going hungry half the time to feed her. They think the little fellow needs me more. You know it would kill me to part with her," said a feeble-minded mother after the birth of her second illegitimate baby when she was advised by an agency to give up the older child. This mother grew up in a sordid home where the only thing which existed in abundance was intemperance of both parents and all the attendant results. Her family was known to a social agency as early as 1903 when this girl was 10 years of age, and up to the present time its different members have received help in one form or another from a dozen agencies, public and private. This girl very naturally became a victim of her environment and gave birth to a child. The first baby she took home where it received as good care as could be expected in such a place. She worked irregularly in a candy factory and earned $5.50 as the highest wage. Ill health and low grade intelligence made it impossible for her ever to hold a good job or to hold any for long. Finally, when the home was broken up at her mother's death, she left. She was employed with her child at a cheap lodging-house when she gave birth to a second child. This woman has struggled along with the two children. For about a year and a half she worked with both at the lodging-house earning $4.00 a week. Illness forced the public authorities to care for mother and children on several occasions. She has received help from time to time, little of it adequate, over a period of years. Only after this woman had given birth to two illegitimate children was she examined by a psychiatrist and found to be definitely feeble-minded and a fit subject for commitment. The children were 9 and 4 years respectively when she became pregnant for a third time by a third man and married him. The last information was that the Overseers of the Poor had agreed to support her, the two illegitimate children, and her husband for a month or two "to get them on their feet." The struggle this mother has made and the hardships she has endured to keep her children would have been considered indicative of character in a person of better intelligence. Society has looked on, now and then giving enough help to keep her miserable body alive, while it has blamed her as a woman of low morals, and done nothing through all these years to safeguard

48

her. Would not the protection afforded by an institution for the feeble-minded or by adequate supervision in the community have been much more humane? Perhaps the burden of taxation which is growing heavier through failure to protect such women and thereby prevent their having offspring will hasten the consummation of plans already conceived.

Attitude of Relatives

It has previously been shown how many of the mothers now found distributed among the three Groups found their way back to their own home or to more remote relatives after a time. Generally speaking, the higher the family standards, the more difficult it has been for its members to receive the mother and her illegitimate child. Some families have helped the mother, but repudiated the child. Undoubtedly, in some cases, relatives hoped that the girl would tire of the idea of keeping the child as soon as she appreciated the ignominy and struggle entailed. When she showed her determination to keep the child even at tremendous cost relatives in some cases relented and took her home, and sometimes the child also. Nearly three years elapsed before the members of one family who really cared for the young mother could bring themselves to receive her and the child.

Helpful to Mother in Keeping Child. Relatives helped make it possible for 28 mothers of Group I to keep the child, by assisting in various ways, but chiefly by taking the mother home. In 5 of these instances they received her without the child.

As a rule, when once the mother went to relatives, particularly parents, she remained with them, usually working outside the home and contributing toward the support of herself and child. Two mothers, exceptions to the rule, illustrate the point that mere reception of mother and child by the family does not necessarily mean satisfactory adjustment. One remained at home but a day or two because of the opposition of one of her brothers. She was then sent to a friend of her mother. There she lived, supporting herself and child, occasionally visiting at home without it, until her marriage. During the past year the child, now living in a distant state with the mother and her husband, visited the maternal grandmother. While not welcomed,

49

the child was at least tolerated by its uncle, who has never forgiven the mother for bringing disgrace to the family. The other mother, who for years before pregnancy had been separated from her family by court action because of parental neglect, remained at home but a few weeks because she objected to the care given the child during the day while she was working at the factory.

In one case only the mother's parents know that she has a child. Although she is one of a large family and returned to her own home after a period of boarding with the child, and although she supports and visits it, she and her parents have succeeded in keeping the secret. In no other instance has the fact of the mother's illegitimate pregnancy probably been known to so few people. One child is supposed to be a boarder in the maternal grandparents' home where she and the mother live. It is said that the facts are known only to the maternal grandmother, but it is suspected that they are known to other members of the family.

Some relatives assisted the mother and child and at the same time made life difficult for the former by their censorious attitude. To illustrate: A respectable woman who feels her daughter's disgrace keenly, gives her a simple but comfortable home. Although devoted to an older child in the home who was the cause of the mother's forced marriage, this maternal grandmother has refused to help with the support of the illegitimate grandchild, will not visit, and even objects to hearing it mentioned. Not to repudiate her responsibility in the face of such unrelenting disapproval shows real affection on the mother's part. If it were not, however, for the material help given by the family in the form of a home for herself and legitimate child, she might be forced to give up the illegitimate now boarded some distance away.

In every instance in which the child has been received by relatives and lived with them long enough to become a member of the family, it has won its way into their affections. Often a family has found it hard to forgive and even more difficult to forget the mother's disgrace, but impossible not to love the innocent victim. In 3 instances it is the maternal grandmother who considers the child her special charge. One has brought him up to regard her as mother and the natural mother as sister. In this case the mother is married and lives under the same roof, but in a different apartment. Another grandmother has had full charge of the child since it was 3 weeks old, the mother continuing to live with them since her marriage. The child knows that the younger woman is her mother, but turns to the older as the more responsible. The third grandmother took the child from the place of confinement ostensibly as a boarder. The mother returned home after a few weeks spent supposedly at work.

Instrumental in Causing Separation. The responsibility for permanent separation rests in 6 cases with relatives. In 2 instances it was the child's maternal grandmother at whose home it was born who gave it away when a few days old. The mother was given no voice in the matter. In the other 4 cases relatives persuaded the mother to part with the child, helped her plan for its disposition, and furnished a considerable sum of money to complete the arrangements. For example, a mother held in an institution awaiting deportation escaped with the child and was with relatives about one month before apprehension. During that time the baby was surrendered to an institution and about $200 deposited by a relative for permanent care. The children disposed of by relatives with one exception were very young babies. The antagonistic attitude of relatives toward keeping the child had its influence on the final decision of more than one mother. There is no discoverable evidence of regret on the part of any family that mother and child were permanently separated; on the contrary there seems to be a feeling that the incident of illegitimacy is closed with the so-called final disposition of the child.

SEX CONDUCT

Marriage a Help in Keeping the Child. Marriage ranked next in importance to relatives as a means of keeping the child. It was of assistance in three ways: First, by restoring the unmarried mother to a respected social status; second, by providing support; third, by establishing a permanent home for mother and child. Of the 24 marriages contracted by the mothers of Group

I during pregnancy or since the child's birth, one-third were with the father. In 20 cases the mother is living with her husband and in 17 has the child with her. Five couples have separated. In 2 of these cases it is the child's father and mother who have separated. In both cases the marriage, unsuccessful in other respects, helped the mother retain the child by restoring a respected social standing. Both girls have self-esteem and are high-grade wage earners of good intelligence, one normal, the other dull normal. They are able to cope with the problem of support without assistance from the child's father. The condemnatory attitude of society towards them as unmarried mothers would be most difficult for them to meet.

The stigma of illegitimacy has been removed from 12 children of this Group, 8 by the belated marriage of the parents, 4 through adoption by the mother's husband. In several other cases adoption is under consideration. It is important to remember that the mother's marriage to someone other than the father does not change the legal status of the child. Adoption by the mother's husband is necessary for legitimization.

Irregular Sex Conduct of Group I. It is interesting to study the conduct of the girls in the light of the theory that keeping the child deters the mother from further sex irregularity. Eleven, more than one-fourth of the 41 mothers of Group I, are known to have had illicit relations since the child's birth as follows: Two of those who finally married the father of the child had relations with at least one other man during the time which elapsed before marriage; 5 became pregnant by and married a man not the father of the child of this study; 1 not pregnant married the second of the two men with whom she is known to have been sexually intimate since the birth of the child; 3 mothers have given birth to a third illegitimate child. Four of those who married a man other than the father and with whom she had had sex relations kept the child with her continuously. Indeed, one of them, the mother of two illegitimate children, had had both with her. Supervision had been particularly good in the case of one of these mothers who had remained at housework with the child under agency care. Only the mother who had the two children with her can be said to have had real difficulty in getting on.

Believers in separation of mother and child may find support of their theory in the fact that 2 of the mothers having a third illegitimate child had kept the older children, the third having parted with one and retained the other.

Eight mothers guilty of illicit relations subsequent to the birth of the child of this study apparently ceased sex irregularity at marriage.

Marriage of Those Separated From Child. One-third of Group II have married, all since the child's birth. Eight couples are living together. Two mothers married the father. In one instance the death of the child united the parents. The father, a widower, had evaded his responsibility and left the burden of support as well as the disgrace to the mother, who had become pregnant while acting as his housekeeper. Her grief at losing the child stirred him. A successful marriage resulted. The woman is making an acceptable stepmother and companion to the man's three children and a good mother to the child born since marriage. The other case is typical of many belated marriages. The man had been arraigned on a charge of bastardy. During a continuance of the case, the marriage took place. There was no basis of affection and no stability of character in man or woman. It was the mother's second illegitimate child. The couple lived together for a few months at the man's home which was already overcrowded by a large family. Then the mother went with her child to her father's home, where she remained until the child died at about 1 year of age. She did her best for the baby and was worn out and grief-stricken at its death. She could have continued to live at her father's comfortable home and have buried the past with the help of her family and her married status, but she chose to return to the old companions. A third illegitimate child by a third man is the result. Marriage in this case served to end the prosecution of the father and to give the child a name. On the other hand it united two people unfitted for family responsibility. It is heartening to find one victim of rape, who was but 13 when attacked by a drunken stepfather, happily married to a young man as wholesome as she. Both joyfully anticipated the birth of their own child. The husband knows of the previous child which was still-born, and holds his wife blameless.

Five of the 8 girls whose second or third illegitimate pregnancy caused her inclusion in this study are married. Two of these contracted a forced marriage when pregnant for the third time, with a man not responsible for either of the previous pregnancies. In one case the mother, of borderline intelligence, had been relieved of both children: of the first by death, of the second by adoption. She married about two years after the birth of the second child and less than one year after parting with it. In the other case the mother, dull normal in intelligence, married a hopeless cripple several years her junior, when she became illegitimately pregnant by him. He was the fourth man with whom she is known to have been sexually irregular. The husband, owing to his physical condition, was dependent upon relatives; the mother, unable to support herself and two children—one of whom she had already kept about five years—allowed the older to be placed for adoption and once more undertook domestic work this time with the legitimate child.

In considering the number of marriages it should be remembered that of the 34 mothers constituting this Group, 2 who have received institutional care continuously since the birth of the child and the 1 who died at childbirth had no opportunity to marry. Moreover, the period during which 4 others were free to marry was shortened, in 1 case by death when the baby was 18 months old, and in 3 by institutional care for a part of the time since confinement.

Irregular Sex Conduct of Group II. Practically 1 of every 3 mothers separated from the child has shown evidence of sex irregularity since confinement. Evidence of further illicit relations is complete in 7 cases, consisting of one mother's own statement, the pregnancy of another, the forced marriage of a third, and illegitimate children born to 4 others. The facts warrant questioning the sex conduct of 5 other mothers. Of those known or suspected of sex delinquency subsequent to confinement, 5 had been illegitimately pregnant at least once before the birth of the child considered in this study. But 1 mother is known to have been sexually irregular after marriage.

54

Marriage and Sex Irregularity of Group III. The meagre data at hand shows that 3 mothers have probably been irregular sexually since the birth of the child. No information has been secured that would indicate marriage for any of this Group.

Marriage and Sex Conduct of Groups I, II, and III. From the facts at hand it appears:

(1) That of the 82 mothers under consideration 35, less than half, are known to have been married at or since the birth of the child here considered. More than half of those who kept the baby, about one-third of those who gave it up, married. The present marital condition of those composing Group III cannot be given. It must be remembered that death and method of treatment precluded the possibility of marriage for some mothers and shortened the period of opportunity for others of Group II, so that it is fair to say that something over half of those in Groups I and II free to marry did so. Marriage came about as early as several months before the child's birth and as late as five and a half years after. The average time which elapsed before marriage was approximately two years, the same for those who kept and those who were separated from the child.

(2) In 1 case in 8 marriage betwen the child's parents occurred. Eight of the 10 mothers who married the father kept the child.

(3) Subsequent to the birth of the child of this study 7 mothers became pregnant by and married someone other than the father. Five of these forced marriages were contracted by those who kept the child.

(4) Group I had 7 mothers free to marry who had been illegitimately pregnant at least once previous to the birth of this child; 1 of these married. Group II had 8 of whom 5 married.

(5) Almost one-fourth of the mothers were "repeaters," *i. e.,* they had been illegitimately pregnant at least once previous to the time of particular concern to this study. Eight are found in Group I, 9 in Group II, 3 in Group III. Sixteen children had already been born to these mothers. Seven "repeaters" continued an irregular sex life with the result that 6 again became pregnant. Nine other individuals, 5 belonging in Group I, whose first experience in unmarried motherhood brought them

within the scope of this study have again become pregnant through illicit relations. The proportion has grown from about one-fourth to more than one-third of the whole until there are 29 who have been illegitimately pregnant at least twice, 10 of them three times. There are facts at hand to warrant the estimate that at least 9 mothers, 6 of them "repeaters" are not living free from irregular sex conduct at the present time. Of this number 3 belong to Group I, 6 to Group II.

(6) A total of 19, nearly one-fourth, are known to have had some irregular sex experience since the child's birth; 11 of Group I, 7 of Group II, 1 of Group III. In addition the sex conduct of 11, of whom 8 belong to Group II, has been open to question at some time since confinement. Forty-two, about half the total number, have led a life apparently free from further irregular sex conduct. Twenty-seven of these have kept the child as compared with 15 who have been separated from it. Care must be taken to give due weight to the fact that death and method of treatment prevented or limited the opportunity for free action on the part of 7 of Group II. It must also be remembered that data is lacking in regard to several of the mothers who have disappeared.

Unmarried motherhood appears less like a problem of the individual and more a matter of community concern when with complete data lacking in several cases it can be stated that up to the present time there are known to have been at least 122 illegitimate pregnancies among 82 mothers resulting in the birth of 111 children.

EMPLOYMENT SUBSEQUENT TO AGENCY CARE

Study of occupation subsequent to agency care shows two points of note: First, only 5 mothers since they have been free to choose their own work are known to have undertaken housework with the child, 3 of Group I, 2 of Group II. It is interesting to discover how small is the number who undertook this work with the child in view of the fact that a third of all the mothers had had some experience in domestic work before confinement, and that the agencies by placing so generally in this employment had not only added to this number but demonstrated the possibility of keeping the child by this occupation. Second, 12 of the 14 classified as "clerks and kindred workers"[1] at the time of application to the agency returned to and remained in the same class of employment when they were free to choose their own work. This shows less change of occupation than occurs in either of the other two classes of gainfully employed. Moreover, one-half this class graded above borderline intelligence, a larger proportion of mothers of better intelligence equipment than existed among those originally classified as "semiskilled workers" or as "servants." More than half of those who returned to the same kind of work had spent from one to four years at high school, taken a business course, or had attended high as well as business school. These mothers, therefore, went back to work for which they were equipped by education which they were able to acquire because of intelligence. Industrial conditions due to the war so increased wages that at least 9 of the factory workers, some of low intelligence, are known to have earned $25 or more a week. This was in excess of the amount earned by the better trained, more purposeful "clerk and kindred workers." Domestic service demanded from $12 to $15 per week. Such wages, of course, give no clue to the economic value of the employee in normal times.

REASONS FOR SEPARATION OF MOTHER AND CHILD

Turning from a consideration of the means by which mothers were enabled to keep the child to the reasons for giving it up, it appears that in 18 of the 34 cases which constitute Group II separation was due to some cause other than agency influence or care. In some instances separation from the child was eagerly sought and the result of voluntary action on the mother's part; in others the cause was beyond her control.

Adoption. Eight children were adopted independently of any agency when under 1 year of age, a like number at about 15 months. The following cases selected from the 8 already referred to show that adoption of the child meant sacrifice and sorrow for some mothers, an easy means of securing freedom

---

[1] This is the same classification as that used by the Children's Bureau in "Illegitimacy as a Child-Welfare Problem," part 2, p. 122.

from an unwelcome burden for others. Two mothers showed reluctance at parting with the child. The first, of dull normal intelligence, whose responsibilities were heavy because she was the oldest of a large number of children, was torn between duty to her family and to the child. After a period of housework with the baby she placed it in an institution in another state. Becoming dissatisfied with its care, she returned to domestic service with it. Again, she became restless. Next she placed the child, then 15 months old, for adoption. Referring to this she said, "Giving it up is not a question of affection but of what I can do." The second mother, feeble-minded, came to this country in early pregnancy. Friends of her family persuaded her to part with the child then a few months old, arranged the adoption, and allowed her to return home. They feel certain that her secret is unknown even to her parents. This mother grieved for the baby, but now finds separation made bearable by the fact that the friends who secured the adoption frequently see it and know that it is well cared for. In contrast to this sorrow at parting with the child and concern for its future welfare, there appears to be a lack of motherly feeling and a callousness as to the child's fate in several cases. For example, another girl of dull normal intelligence, kept the child at her father's home for a short time, then placed it at board and was content to allow it to be adopted through the boarding home at 15 months without knowing the identity of the adoptive parents or anything about them. Still another mother, feeble-minded, with two illegitimate children, showed no reluctance at giving both children for adoption. No relation is apparent between the mother's affection for the child and her intelligence. Other illustrations could be given to show that the feeble-minded, the normal, and those grading between have parted with the child, reluctantly in some cases, eagerly in others.

What of the homes into which these children have gone? What kind of stock has been transplanted? Insufficient information makes it impossible to answer the first question. In reply to the second it can be said that the psychiatric examination graded the intelligence of the mothers of 6 of these 8 children as follows: 2 dull normal, 2 borderline, 2 feeble-minded. The other 2 mothers were unclassified as to intelligence because they did not cooperate in the tests. One was "emotionally unstable, strongly antagonistic, and paranoid and secretive," but "apparently of fair intelligence." The other was "hysterical, secretive and depressed; not graded by intelligence tests because of her emotional inability to cooperate."

The need already indicated (p. 41) of some authoritative supervision which would guarantee reasonable care for all illegitimate children and prevent disposition according to the whim of a mother who may be feeble-minded, insane, or otherwise unfit, or who is bound to be relieved of her responsibility regardless of the welfare of the child, becomes again apparent when it is found that 8 of the 13 children known to have been adopted were placed with prospective adoptive parents without investigation by agency or person competent to make this delicate social adjustment.

The New York State Charities Aid Association has recently completed a six months' study of advertisements appearing in New York papers offering children for adoption to anyone who applies for them and advertisements seeking children to "adopt." The study shows that children are often taken from their mothers without legal formalities, that they are frequently returned and passed from person to person and "in some cases all traces of the identity of the child are lost and it has not a vestige of legal standing during the coming years." Some of the conclusions are interesting: "It is clear that large numbers of unmarried mothers are surrendering their babies to strangers about whose morals, personality, financial standing and standards of living they know nothing * * * that children of unknown history and family traits who are possibly feeble-minded, psychopathic or tainted with inherited disease, are being foisted upon ignorant but in many cases well-meaning foster parents; that such indiscriminate giving away of children not only works great hardships upon individual children and individual foster parents, but also has the effect of discrediting conscientious and intelligent home-finding done by competent child-placing agencies."[1] In New

---

[1] *New York State Charities Aid News* April, 1922.

York "the careless giving away of children" is not illegal, neither is it in Massachusetts.

Death of Child. Six children died subsequent to agency care, 4 while at board, 2 with the mother. All under 2 years and 4 were under 1 year at time of death.

Death of Mother. Death of the mother brought about the separation from a child of 18 months who was surrendered to an institution by surviving relatives.

Inadequate Supervision and Its Results

It is probable that close follow-up work would have prevented at least 2 feeble-minded mothers from legally abandoning the child after securing public care for it. These mothers were unable to carry the whole burden but could have shared it, as they agreed to do, with the taxpayer to the moral advantage of the one and the financial advantage of the other. One of these feeble-minded mothers who had already kept her child two and a half years visited it for a few months after placing, then disappeared. It is nearly three years since her whereabouts were known. The other mother, whose last interest in the child of whom she formerly seemed so fond was evinced some eighteen months ago, was found working in a state institution as an attendant where her husband to whom she was married after placement of the child is also employed. The total income of the couple is over $1,500 and living, a sum sufficient to enable them to support the child. A staff of workers adequate in number and not overburdened with work as at present, would have permitted the agency to keep in sufficiently close touch with this woman to note her improved financial and social status and to adjust the burden of the child's care and support accordingly.

The fact that a considerable number of these mothers were unable to get along without agency help in addition to that received in connection with the birth of the child seems to bear out the contention that a longer period of supervision was desirable.

Following the termination of care by the agency responsible for the case at confinement 27 mothers, nearly one-third the total number, are known to have made further demand upon society for some form of assistance through agencies public and private.

In several instances the same individual has been the recipient of care from more than one source. For example, a mother venereally diseased who again became illegitimately pregnant and was finally committed to a penal institution received medical care for disease and confinement and treatment of a punitive nature from the court. Medical care for the mother was a form of help given in 14 cases, in 10 of which it was made necessary by further sex irregularity manifested by venereal disease or some result of it, by another illegitimate pregnancy, or both.

The courts have dealt with 4 girls, committing 2 to reformatories, one upon complaint of her mother driven to this course in a vain attempt to prevent another illegitimate pregnancy. Probation was given in 2 instances with the understanding that 1 mother was to spend her term as a voluntary inmate of an institution. It was a sex offense in 3 of the 4 cases which made court action necessary. In a few instances a socially-minded probation officer has supervised mother and child for many months while collecting money under court order from the man adjudged the father. Material relief has been necessary in a few cases for short periods.

Additional assistance was needed by 11 children whose mothers had been discharged from agency care but were unable to carry the burden without further help. The service rendered these children varied from hospital treatment given over a short period to an assumption of care with the probability of permanency. At the present time society is known to be contributing through voluntary gifts or taxation partial support of 6 children, full support of 7. Nine of these 13 children have been in agency care since birth.

It is well to note that 6 of the 10 mothers who made additional medical care necessary by further sex irregularity were feeble-minded, while one other was psychoneurotic.

The case of one mother, 16 when the child was born and feeble-minded, demands special mention because it illustrates the way in which many a girl unable to manage her own life and with no one to direct it for her, now and then compels society to pay for its neglect. Upon examination the psychiatrist wrote, "Girl is dull, but it must be noticed that she has always been undernourished and has had no fair chance * * * an ignorant, half-starved little girl, pale and anemic." Her family has been known to sixteen social agencies over a period of twenty years. The mental examination pointed out her great need of protection. The man responsible for her condition was her employer, nearly three times her age, married and with children of his own. His wife and this girl were confined at the same hospital within a few weeks of each other. Since that time this unmarried mother has given birth to two other children by him. Following the birth of the third the girl was placed in an institution for several months under strict discipline. The man was prosecuted after the birth of the first child, and although he has been under court order for several years and was finally given a suspended sentence to a correctional institution after his third offense, he has not been deprived of his liberty. If this girl from early childhood had been protected and trained by care in a school for the feeble-minded or by close supervision in the community, how different the story might have been! This is but one of several mothers of this study who needed protection over a period of years and failed to obtain it.

SUMMARY

Eighty-two women selected because each (1) became illegitimately pregnant and gave birth to a child from three to six years previous to the period of the study; (2) was assisted by some social agency because of this; (3) was given a psychiatric examination in the course of social treatment, are grouped according to whether they have kept the child, been permanently separated from it, or disappeared with it.

This arrangement makes possible a comparison of the mother who has carried her responsibility with the one who has shirked or been involuntarily relieved of it.

One-half of these women have kept the child, 34 have been separated from it, 7 have disappeared with it.

TREATMENT

While in individual cases mother and child were separated because of mental defect or disease which was discovered by the psychiatric examination, no attempt was made to cause every feeble-minded or mentally disordered mother to part with the child. Therefore, mothers of every grade of intelligence still have the child, while others also representing every grade of intelligence have been separated from it. No relation is apparent between the mother's intelligence and her affection for her offspring. All who have dropped out of sight with the child are unclassified or below the borderline grade of intelligence.

The agencies undertook treatment on the assumption that each mother was to keep her child, and assisted her to do so until persuaded that separation was warranted by the facts of the particular case. Separation was decided upon after periods varying from less than a month after confinement to more than five years. About one-fourth of those who are separated from the child kept it for a considerable period, in one case more than five years.

63

With Relatives. Following confinement the agencies attempted to re-establish the mother as a member of her own family group whenever possible and desirable.

More than half the total number of mothers—five-eighths of them with the child—were finally in the home of parents or relatives.

In Employment. The agencies provided employment for the majority of mothers who did not go to relatives and for those whose return was delayed.

A little less than half of Groups I and II and one-third of Group III were placed at work, more than four-fifths of them with the child. Housework and wet nursing were the only occupations offered as a first job. At the expiration of one year after the first placement approximately two-thirds of the mothers placed by an agency had ceased to work with the child. Two-thirds of those who continued a year or more in the occupation provided belong to Group I.

After a period at housework or wet nursing the agencies usually approved of mothers attempting other work and assisted or allowed them to find it.

Special training was given to but 1 of every 16 mothers.

The services rendered by agencies in addition to the more usual ones just mentioned are of great importance and may be expected to increase in variety as the treatment of the unmarried mother becomes less stereotyped.

Marriage. The agencies helped to bring about marriage in only a few cases. Apparently it was seldom regarded as desirable unless there seemed to be a reasonable likelihood of some happiness and of the establishment of a home suitable for the upbringing of the child.

Separation of Mother and Child. Agencies were largely responsible for approximately one-third the total number of separations which occurred. Practically half the children separated from the mother through agency influence were legally adopted, the other half placed in public care.

Supervision. It has been impossible to fix an average time during which the agencies exercised supervision owing to the indefiniteness of many case records on this point and to the lack of uniformity in the use of the term. Oversight more or less intensive was continued in the majority of cases until there seemed to be reason to feel that the mother could get on without agency help or that further effort on her behalf would be futile.

The supervision given the members of Groups I and II does not seem to differ. There are mothers who have kept the child and others who have been separated from it who received wise, intensive oversight over a period of many months. On the other hand there are individuals in both Groups who received almost no oversight after leaving the place of confinement. Group III as a whole received less oversight than either of the others. The responsibility for nearly half of Group III was transferred following confinement to public officials, federal and state, who arranged for deportation or return to out-of-state authorities. Other mothers needed but did not desire supervision from any source and soon dropped out of sight.

The mothers of all Groups received practically the same treatment due probably in large measure to the fact that the ultimate goal of the agencies was keeping mother and child together and that separation was advocated only as a last resort. At present there seem to be but a limited number of things which agencies are doing for the unmarried mother. More flexibility of treatment will undoubtedly develop with greater understanding of the real need of the individual and of the problem.

SUBSEQUENT HISTORY

The latest information obtainable shows that 2 of the 82 mothers of the study have died, the present whereabouts of 9 are unknown, 2 legally abandoning the child, 7 disappearing with it. Of the remainder all but 2 are in the community. A little more than one-fourth of the feeble-minded of the study are receiving oversight, some of it superficial, from various sources. In other words, approximately three-fourths of the feeble-minded are in the community unsupervised.

Occupation. When the mothers were free to select employment:

(1) Only a very small proportion went to housework with the child.

(2) Six-sevenths of those employed as "clerks or kindred workers" at the time of pregnancy went back to that class of work and remained in it.

Half the mothers included in this classification were above the borderline grade of intelligence—a higher proportion of mothers of better intelligence than appears among those designated as "semiskilled" or as "servants." It is apparent that there has been less changing from one classification of work to another among those of better intelligence.

Attitude of Relatives. While the relations existing between the mother and her family since confinement have not always been helpful or cordial, it is evident that relatives have played an important part in deciding whether the mother should keep the child or be permanently parted from it.

In more than two-thirds of the cases in which the mother kept the child relatives helped to make it possible. In the largest number of instances they assisted by giving the mother a home at least for a time. In more than four-fifths of these cases the baby was permitted to accompany the mother.

Relatives, on the other hand, were largely responsible for permanent separation of mother and child in about 1 case in every 6 where it occurred.

SEPARATION OF MOTHER AND CHILD

Slightly more than half the total number of separations occurred apart from agency care or influence.

Adoption was arranged for parctically 1 child in every 4 separated from its mother by individuals interested primarily in disposing of it. Whether the adoptive homes were suitable, what has been the fate of these children, is not known. The important fact is that there is no agency in Massachusetts charged with the responsibility of making an investigation to determine the fitness of a prospective adoption from the point of view of the child, its mother, and the adoptive parents. When it is considered that under agency auspices and independently something over one-third the total number of children permanently separated from the mother—almost one-sixth of all the children of the study—have been legally adopted, it becomes apparent that adoption is a method frequently used in disposing of illegitimate children.

Death. About 1 child in every 8 of the study has died—twice as many since as during agency care. All of these children were under 2 years of age, four-fifths under 1 year at the time of death.

The facts relating to adoption and death indicate the need of authority which would enable the State to exercise supervision over all its illegitimate children and thereby prevent "the placing of a child for adoption, the transferring of guardianship, or the permanent placement for care without order of the court or State Department made after investigation."

RELATION OF SECRECY TO SOCIAL REHABILITATION

Secrecy which is sometimes regarded as the unmarried mother's protection has been maintained so completely in a few cases as to exclude close relatives from a knowledge of the mother's experience. Thus the girl is enmeshed in a web of deception which is a tremendous handicap to social rehabilitation. Moreover, the effect on the individual of constant fear of discovery and repression may be serious. The mothers who are struggling to keep the child under these circumstances seem to be carrying a heavier burden than any others of the study. Apparently they are facing disgrace aggravated by long-practiced deception should the facts become known, deep sorrow at parting with the child after years of real sacrifice to maintain it should they decide upon separation, or an indefinite period of more worry, sacrifice, and deception.

SEX

Keeping the child has not deterred approximately one-fourth of the mothers of Group I from further sex irregularity. On the other hand about one-fifth of those who have been "relieved of the burden of the support and complications which an illegitimate child entails" have also had illicit relations since the birth of the child of the study resulting in 5 additional illegitimate pregnancies. More than two-thirds of those known to have been sexually irregular since confinement and almost three-fourths of those suspected of being, are below the dull normal grade of intelligence, unclassified, or suffering from some psychic disorder.

These facts seem to indicate that the mother's intelligence and mental health are important factors in her ability to control her sex activity.

Marriage. Less than half the mothers of the study are married, about one-half of Group I, approximately one-third of Group II. Data is lacking concerning Group III.

Marriage must be regarded as a powerful stabilizer as is demonstrated by two facts: (1) More than six-sevenths of those mothers who married subsequent to the birth of the child seem to have lived free from suspicion of sex irregularity since marriage. A considerable number of these were known to have had illicit relations between confinement and marriage. (2) The mothers who are considered to be better adjusted socially at present than when pregnancy occurred are with few exceptions married.

Responsibility and love for the child unquestionably play an important part in the life of many unmarried mothers, but these factors evidently do not entirely keep the sex life within the bounds prescribed by society.

III. GENERAL CONCLUSIONS, TABLES AND CHARTS

Without regard to the method of treatment or any inter-current circumstance and taking only the bare facts which emerge from Miss Parker's investigation, let us see where the 82 unmarried mothers stand after the lapse of approximately five years. What we wish to know, naturally, indeed all that we can know, is how they have turned out from the viewpoint of society. We cannot, of course, gauge the subtle internal or psychic effect on their own personality or character, nor the indirect and remote effect on society that will not become evident until the children of these mothers become active elements in the community. We can take account only of such material, external, and immediate effects as we can see. As in all purely social evaluations, we must judge by outward signs alone.

Proceeding from this objective standpoint, we have singled out certain particulars that are commonly considered indicative of social worth in the individual, namely, occupational and economic status, or what the girl works at and earns; moral and social status, or how the girl acts, that is, whether she abides by the law and the accepted social standards; and, because of its peculiar relation to this problem, marital status. On the basis of these particulars combined under the head of social status, we have attempted to decide, after a careful weighing of each girl's record, whether at the time the investigation closed she had a better, a worse, or the same social status that she had at the time the experience came to her.

We have also attempted to discern whether by this experience of motherhood without marriage she has injured or not appreciably affected society. (There was no evidence that she had bettered society.) Here again, we can take account only of the direct and tangible injury brought to the community, such as expense of one sort or another over and above that for mere confinement (this is assumed to be a normal province of the agencies), for prolonged hospital or institutional care for mother or child, for public or private care of the child, for law procedures;

69

or such social inquiry as the disrupting of family relationships either in the girl's own family or in that of the partner; undue scandal in the neighborhood; death of the girl from causes depending on the fact of pregnancy; etc.

It can readily be seen that the outcome to the girl and the outcome to society are not necessarily the same. For example, a girl through being an unmarried mother, may occasion much expense to the community for hospital and other care for herself and child, for prosecution of the partner, and for other items: yet if later the child having been given for adoption or to an agency, the girl marries and betters her social condition, although the community is considerably out of pocket the girl herself at the moment of our inquiry is clearly a better social asset than she was when she came into the initial study.

In making our conclusions as to the social readjustment, or as we term it "the social status," we have been forced to adopt arbitrary definitions as to what was better, worse, and the same in order to make our decisions uniform and comparable and always from the objective standpoint. Without such definition we found ourselves shifting from objective to subjective evaluations: interpreting sometimes on the basis of social evidence and sometimes on what we happened to know or thought we knew of the girl's ethical and moral principle and force of character. Accordingly, we had to eliminate all attempt to measure outcome in terms of abstract attributes and to limit ourselves solely to what we could see of her social reactions and circumstances. In order to be clear as to what we mean by *better, worse,* and *same* we illustrate: A girl who was married and living in an established home in an apparently satisfactory way with her husband, we considered a *better* social unit. A girl married but separated or divorced and without an established home and generally occupying a less respected or a less influential position, we considered a *worse* social unit even though she may have shown force of character in sacrificing her own interests to that of her child; also a girl in an institution or wholly or partly dependent on an agency for support or one in any way functioning on a lower social plane than she was at the time she entered into our initial study, we placed in the category of *worse*. A girl who gave

70

away her child or had it assimilated by her own family and went on with her daily life as if nothing had happened and without apparent change in her conduct or external circumstances, we considered the *same* social unit.

The conclusions are presented in the tables and charts which follow. Because mental status has been made the underlying motif of this study, the tables and charts have been arranged so as to show results in relation to the various mental diagnoses.

TABLE I

TABLE SHOWING THE PRESENT SOCIAL STATUS OF 82 UNMARRIED MOTHERS COMPARED WITH THE SOCIAL STATUS AT THE TIME OF PREGNANCY (APPROXIMATELY FIVE YEARS PREVIOUSLY) ARRANGED ACCORDING TO THE MENTAL DIAGNOSIS

Intelligence	Better	Same	Worse	Un-known	Died	Total
Normal I. Q. 105 to 90	6	2	1	0	0	9
Dull normal I. Q. 89 to 80	7	8	4	0	0	19
Borderline I. Q. 79 to 70	5	8	4	2	1	20
Feeble-minded I. Q. 69 to 50	6	7	5	5	0	23
Unclassified I. Q. not certain	4	2	2	2	1	11
Total	28	27	16	9	2	82
Psychopathic (Psychotic, Psycho- neurotic, Epileptic) ..	3	1	4	2	1	11

71

CHART I (TABLE I)

SHOWING PRESENT SOCIAL STATUS (THE PERCENTAGES OF THE VARIOUS
INTELLIGENCE GRADES ARE INSERTED)

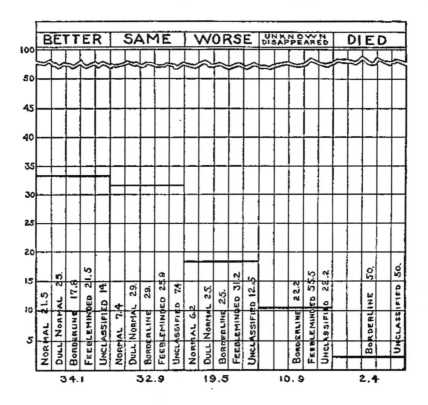

CHART IA (TABLE I)

SHOWING THE DISTRIBUTION OF THE PRESENT SOCIAL STATUS IN THE
VARIOUS MENTAL DIAGNOSES

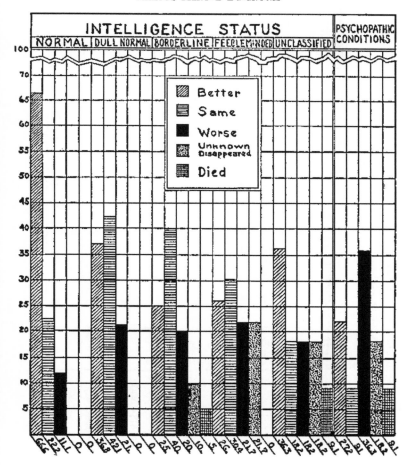

TABLE II

Table Showing the Apparent Effect on the Community of the Occurrence of 82 Cases of Motherhood Without Marriage Distributed According to Mental Diagnosis

Effect on Community	INTELLIGENCE GRADE						Psychopathic incl. Psychotic, Psychoneurotic, Epileptic
	Normal I. Q. 105-90	Dull normal I. Q. 89-80	Borderline I. Q. 79-70	Feeble-minded I. Q. 69-50	Unclassified I. Q. ?	Total	
Good	0	0	0	0	0		0
Bad	4	5	10	17	8	44	10
No apparent effect	5	14	8	6	3	36	1
Unknown (disappeared)	0	0	2	0	0	2	
Total	9	19	20	23	11	82	11

CHART II (TABLE II)
SHOWING THE APPARENT EFFECT ON THE COMMUNITY IN RELATION TO THE
VARIOUS MENTAL DIAGNOSES

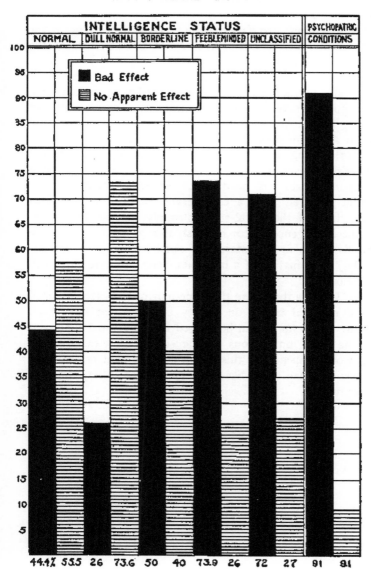

With less than one-fifth of the group occupying after a relatively brief lapse of time a social position worse than at the time the experience came to them, it would appear that the incident of maternity without marriage had not played the havoc in the life of the individual that the accounts of the novelists or the ominous regard of society would lead one to expect. Yet, surely, no reader would possibly see in this an implication that for a woman to have a child without being married was an easy or a desirable thing. There are, as anyone can see, many intricate and far-reaching ramifications of the subject which to discuss would lead too far afield for present purposes. If the selective character of the cases figuring in this study is kept in mind, as indeed the repeated reiteration of it must insure, there is little danger that misleading inferences will be drawn. Nevertheless, it must be added, data gathered from a considerable number of examinations since those of the initial study strongly suggest that, in respect to the intelligence factor at least, this group may be more representative than in the interest of strict accuracy we can assume. Only examination of a large number of routine cases will settle this point.

Table II shows that more than one-half of the cases inflicted visible and material injury on society in ways that have been pointed out. In so far as can be judged from outward signs and in so far as effect on persons can be compared with effect on society it would appear, for this group at least, that motherhood without marriage had more disastrous import for society than for the mother herself.